MAURIZIO LA CAVA

STARTUP PITCH PRESENTATION

THE ULTIMATE METHODOLOGY TO CREATING A BRILLIANT STARTUP PITCH PRESENTATION AND WIN FUNDING

STARTUP PITCH PRESENTATION

THE ULTIMATE METHODOLOGY TO CREATING A BRILLIANT STARTUP PITCH PRESENTATION AND WIN FUNDING

Find me on the web at https://mauriziolacava.com
To report errors, please send a note to maurizio@mauriziolacava.com

Editor & Proofreader: Holly Hunt

Book Layout & Cover Designer: Anna Magmel

Notice of Rights

All rights reserved. This book was self-published by the author Maurizio La Cava. No part of this book may be reproduced in any form by any means without the express permission of the author. This includes reprints, excerpts, photocopying, recording, or any future means of reproducing text

Notice of Liability

The information in this book is distributed on an "As Is" basis without warranty. While every precaution has been taken in the preparation of the book, the author shall have any liability to any person or entity with respect to any loss or damage caused or alleged to be caused directly or indirectly by the instructions contained in this book or by the computer software and hardware product described in it

CONTENTS

INTRODUCTION **8**

1. STARTUP, PITCH & FUNDRAISING 10

1.1 Being entrepreneurs is a vocation 12
1.2 Communicate to survive 13
1.3 Everyone "pitches", or must learn to do it 15
1.4 The financing route of a startup 16
1.5 Managing expectations – the Venture Capital funnel 20
1.6 Why should a pitch fail? 23
    1.6.1 Failure to establish an immediate connection 23
    1.6.2 Having a badly structured pitch 24
    1.6.3 Not understanding the audience 25
    1.6.4 Not understanding your market 25
    1.6.5 Not knowing your competitors 26
    1.6.6 Revealing an incomplete team 26
    1.6.7 Revealing weak financials or an excessive request 26
1.7 Summarizing 27

2. GET TO KNOW WHO IS IN FRONT OF YOU 28

2.1 Analyze your audience 30
    2.1.1 Your audience is the hero 32
    2.1.2 People act in a selfish way 33
    2.1.3 What are investors looking for? 34
2.2 The first impression is what really counts 37
    2.2.1 Pushover 38
    2.2.2 Robot 38
    2.2.3 Second hand car salesman 39
    2.2.4 Beggar 40
2.3 Catch attention 42
2.4 Learn how to manage interactions 46
2.5 Summarizing 49

3. HOW TO PERSUADE THE AUDIENCE — 50

3.1 Persuasion techniques — 52
3.2 Practical guide to persuasion — 53
    3.2.1 Credibility — 53
    3.2.2 Focus on the audience — 58
    3.2.3 Emotionality — 59
3.3 Storytelling for presentations — 66
3.4 Four techniques to definitely "not persuade" — 70
    3.4.1 Being impatient — 70
    3.4.2 Do not accept compromise — 70
    3.4.3 Acting in a short-term approach — 71
    3.4.4 Believe that the presentation is everything — 72
3.5 Summarizing — 73

4. THE PITCH: AN EFFICIENT STRUCTURE — 74

4.1 Investor pitch or business plan? — 76
    4.1.1 Business plan — 76
    4.1.2 Investor pitch — 76
4.2 What is an elevator pitch? — 78
4.3 What information to include in a pitch — 81
4.4 The perfect structure for a successful investor pitch — 86
4.5 Summarizing — 87

5. THE PROBLEM — 88

5.1 Give the people what they want — 90
5.2 The problem as an integral part of storytelling — 91
5.3 Problem, pain and consequences — 93
5.4 When the problem doesn't exist yet — 95
5.5 Persuasion applied to the problem — 97
    5.5.1 Credibility — 97
    5.5.2 Focus on the audience — 98
    5.5.3 Emotionality — 99
5.6 Summarizing — 101

6. THE SOLUTION — 102

6.1 Unique value proposition	104
6.2 Demo: shall I do it or not?	106
6.3 The solution as saving	108
6.4 Persuasion applied to the solution	109
6.4.1 Credibility	109
6.4.2 Focus on the audience	111
6.4.3 Emotionality	111
6.5 Summarizing	113

7. MARKET SIZE — 114

7.1 Predicting the future looking at the trends?	117
7.2 From potential to served market	118
7.3 Be ambitious and forget the VC	119
7.4 Bottom up vs Top down	120
7.5 The Market Niche concept and why we like it	122
7.6 Persuasion applied to Market Size	123
7.6.1 Credibility	123
7.6.2 Focus on the audience	123
7.6.3 Emotionality	125
7.7 Summarizing	127

8. BUSINESS MODEL — 128

8.1 What is a business model	130
8.2 Business model canvas	132
8.3 Sustainability of the business model	135
8.4 A pitch business model	137
8.5 Persuasion applied to business model	140
8.5.1 Credibility	140
8.5.2 Focus on the audience	141
8.5.3 Emotionality	141
8.6 Summarizing	143

9. TRACTION — 144

9.1 Metrics and common mistakes — 146
9.2 Persuasion applied to traction — 149
    9.2.1 Credibility — 149
    9.2.2 Focus on the audience — 149
    9.2.3 Emotionality — 150
9.3 Summarizing — 151

10. COMPETITION — 152

10.1 Unique, indeed, but in the way of doing it! — 154
10.2 Porter's 5 strengths model — 158
10.3 What does competition look like? — 162
10.4 Persuasion applied to competition — 164
    10.4.1 Credibility — 164
    10.4.2 Focus on the audience — 164
    10.4.3 Emotionality — 165
10.5 Summarizing — 167

11. GO-TO-MARKET — 168

11.1 Make things happen — 170
11.2 Let's introduce Go-to-market — 171
11.3 Persuasion applied to Go-to-market — 173
    11.3.1 Credibility — 173
    11.3.2 Focus on the audience — 173
    11.3.3 Emotionality — 174
11.4 Summarizing — 175

12. THE TEAM — 176

12.1 Small and well stocked — 178
12.2 The ideal team slide — 180
12.3 Persuasion applied to the team — 183
    12.3.1 Credibility — 183
    12.3.2 Focus on the audience — 183
    12.3.3 Emotionality — 184
12.4 Summarizing — 185

13. FINANCIAL PROJECTIONS — 186

- 13.1 Realize consistent projections — 188
- 13.2 Predicting the future is not easy — 189
- 13.3 Project your ambition — 190
- 13.4 A map that can show you the way — 191
- 13.5 Present the financial projections — 192
- 13.6 Persuasion applied to financial projections — 193
    - 13.6.1 Credibility — 193
    - 13.6.2 Focus on the audience — 194
    - 13.6.3 Emotionality — 194
- 13.7 Summarizing — 195

14. CALL TO ACTION — 196

- 14.1 Ask and you will receive — 198
- 14.2 What to ask (real life examples) — 200
- 14.3 Persuasion applied to call to action — 201
    - 14.3.1 Credibility — 201
    - 14.3.2 Focus on the audience — 201
    - 14.3.3 Emotionality — 202
- 14.4 Summarizing — 205

15. ROADMAP — 206

- 15.1 One step at a time — 208
- 15.2 Presenting the roadmap — 211
- 15.3 Persuasion applied to the roadmap — 213
    - 15.3.1 Credibility — 213
    - 15.3.2 Focus on the audience — 213
    - 15.3.3 Emotionality — 214
- 15.4 Summarizing — 215

16. END WITH A CONTACTS SLIDE — 216

- 16.1 Investor pitch canvas — 218
- 16.2 The role of graphics in a presentation to the investors — 221

+ GET YOUR FREE BONUSES! — 222

- Bibliography — 224
- Sitography — 225
- University papers and articles — 227

0
CHAPTER

INTRODUCTION

Every startupper has to create an effective pitch for his activity, his product or service to win over an audience.

The pitch could be a sales presentation to potential customers, a presentation to offer a strategic partnership to another company or the usual presentation to raise funds.

Unlike all the other presentations, a pitch to raise funds has specific critical points. The Pitch is a presentation that can easily decide the success or failure of a business initiative.

If the pitch works well, the company gains the financial resources to sustain itself and, hopefully, grow, otherwise it might fail for lack of resources.

However, producing a pitch is a hard activity. We are not talking about the usual presentation, as the main aim is to persuade a specific target audience: investors specialized in the analysis of investment opportunities in startups.

Investors are used to identifying a business opportunity in a very short time, this is why your chances are minimized and you can't allow yourself to make mistakes.

Moreover, entrepreneurs that present a pitch to investors often have to respect very short time limits. On many occasions entrepreneurs are timed during their presentation and are stopped if they don't finish on time.

This is when we start having doubts: what does the investor want to see in my slides? What could he ask me that I haven't said? How should I present information in order to obtain an effective flow? How can I prevent my audience from falling asleep during my presentation? Which parts of the pitch must be shown and which ones can be omitted? Are there any models that can help me create and produce the contents of my presentation?

In this book I will show the result of the analysis of many personal experiences in this field, that led me to produce a standard structure, complete and well-organized, of all the sections that must be included in an investor pitch presentation.

The first part of the book concentrates on the science of persuasion applied to pitch presentations. I will then talk about the analysis and communication structure of every good investor pitch. The final part will focus on each section of the pitch, with practical examples taken from the most successful pitches around.

Among blogs and specialized books, there's a lot of confusion about the structure that should be used to create an investor pitch.

Due to the absence, in Italy and abroad, of a unique presentation structure, that is clear and well defined, I decided to analyze the information available online and in literature to create a benchmark structure, that would be effective and easy to use.

Thanks to the application of this new structure, your will be able to create effective investor pitches much more quickly than before. The speed won't affect the quality, which is why the detailed structure I describe will include all the sections of a pitch that must, absolutely, be included in your presentation.

This way you will have a point of reference, a powerful instrument that will increase the effectiveness and completeness of your future presentations to investors.

1
CHAPTER

STARTUP, PITCH & FUNDRAISING

Making pitch presentations to raise funds is an art, a profession; it's the continuous challenge of being an entrepreneur.

Being an entrepreneur means working with passion to develop your startup and ensure its survival. It's said that 1 startup out of 10 is intended to fail, and one of the causes is the incapacity of communicating our project (pitching) and staying within the adequate fundraising funnel.

Why should you decide to become an entrepreneur; what are the pros and cons of this profession that is becoming so popular lately? What are the challenges of fundraising and why is it so important, and at the same time so difficult, to communicate?

1.1 BEING AN ENTREPRENEUR IS A VOCATION

The world is changing rapidly and it's getting easier to gain access to skills, technologies and funding. Entrepreneurship is starting to become a real professional alternative to traditional career paths.

Everyone in the world is talking about startups and in Italy this word is becoming more and more popular. The media are focusing attention on the ever-growing business environment, investments are increasing and startuppers are part of an increasingly dense network of professions, ideas and innovative projects.

But why should you prefer to be a startupper rather than a manager in a multinational business, after years of studying hard and a degree from a prestigious university?

They say a startupper can work wherever he wants, manage rhythms and workloads in whichever way he likes, without ever having to refer to a boss who will manage his daily timetable for the rest of his life.

Although I agree that these features characterize the modern entrepreneur, you must consider that, as for everything, there are pros and cons.

It's true that you can work remotely from any place you choose, but I can assure you, from my own experience, that the beach is not necessarily the best place to organize a Skype call with a customer.

Of course, you manage your own workloads, but when you stop, so do all your business activities, which means you always need to be in contact and operative, unless you want to put everything on hold until you get back to the office.

After all, although it may be true you haven't got a boss to refer to, most probably, you'll have customers with whom the dynamics of negotiation for delivery time and terms can be very similar to – or even worse than – those you would have with a boss.

Also, what about money? Do you prefer a fixed, secure salary each month, or a precarious insecurity for the rest of your life?

So, why do more and more young people choose to follow this path instead of others?

Apart from changing trends, I think that doing business is a need, and not a choice. I think that people who are born with this vocation can feel it inside themselves and, even though they can ignore it for some time, sooner or later it will bloom and change their lives forever.

After all, resisting change and refusing to listen to your inner voice would mean giving up your dreams to a life of privations.

> *"If you don't build your dream, someone will hire you to help to build theirs".*
>
> **Tony Gaskins**

1.2 COMMUNICATE TO SURVIVE

If you're reading this book, I assume that you, like myself, could not resist the call and decided to start a business.

I don't know what you think, but I remember the scary statistics of the mortality rate of startups when I first started. Depending on your field, the rate can be a little different, but in the end, according to Forbes, more than 90% of startups fail.[1]

The reasons are many: the team wasn't able to manage the project, the funds ran out so production stopped, a competitor was better and faster than you and conquered the market from under your nose, etc.

In this book, I would like to concentrate on the most frequent reason for failure - the inability to communicate your project and get funded.

To produce an effective pitch is the second most difficult thing to realize for a startupper, the first one is to create something people really want!

"Many startups fail because they are not capable of creating a really useful product, but the second reason of failure is probably the incapacity of raising funds. Fundraising is brutal".[2]

Paul Grahm

According to Paul Graham, there are three reasons for this brutality:

THE MARKET IS BRUTAL

Unlike those who live in academic or corporate environments, where you pay for your mistakes but you always find a way out, the market doesn't forgive.

If you think about it, if you fail an exam you can retake it, you can refuse a bad mark which you don't like, and at the annual evaluation with your boss, if something goes wrong, you can always do better next year, and you will always have some strong points in your favor to balance the weak points. When you're out on the market, however, you haven't got a second chance; if your product doesn't really solve the problems of the people who are interested in it, they won't buy it and no one will give you a second chance.

THERE ARE LESS INVESTORS THAN CUSTOMERS

Investors judge your startup with the same brutal logic used by customers to judge your product: if they're not convinced, they will pass! The fact is, potential investors are very few compared to potential customers, and this reduces your chances of being funded.

If, on the market, you can lose customers without risking your whole business, when you are raising funds, the success of your pitch can define the destiny of your startup. Talking to investors is a precious opportunity and you must make the most of it.

---

[1] Patel N., 90% of startups fail: here's what you need to know about the 10%, forbes.com
[2] A fundraising survivor guide, paulgraham.com

INVESTORS WORK IN UNDEFINED CONTEXTS

Investors have to make decisions about funding projects, but they often don't understand all the projects that they analyze and in which they invest. For this reason, when you raise funds, you might find yourself among a team of people interested in the outcome of your project, but who don't understand the logic of your business.

This is why you will be faced with few investors, with unclear ideas, whom you must convince to fund your idea.

So, in such a complex and challenging environment, knowing how to transmit your ideas in the best way possible is essential. You can't afford to make mistakes.

Why is learning how to present your project so important?

Because an excellent project with a poor presentation might be overshadowed by a poor project presented in an excellent way. Often, a pitch presentation occurs in a stressful situation and very little time is available, but on those occasions, you will have a great opportunity to connect with your audience.

> **Nancy Duarte says:**
>
> *"Presentations create a catalyst for meaningful change by using human contact in a way that no other medium can".*
>
> *"Often, until you talk to people, you can't create the visceral connection that will get people to adopt your ideas".*[3]

One of the responsibilities of being founder or co-founder of a startup is that you must know how to communicate your projects to customers, investors, friends and anyone else!

Let's put it this way: you can have the best idea in the world, but if you're not able to transmit it properly, the chance of your project failing is very high.

The starting point in the funding process of a startup is the project pitch. This is the moment when entrepreneurs and investors first come into contact. During this time entrepreneurs present their pitch, in order to persuade investors to fund their startup.

Investor pitches are often very competitive presentations, with a very short time available and precise rules to follow. During these presentations, the smallest mistake can be fatal. The consequence of a bad pitch presentation is that investors will not fund your activity, and you might find yourself without enough money to keep your project alive.

Failing to transmit your ideas is essentially a free ticket to join the 90% of startups that didn't make it.

---

[3] Duarte N. Resonate - Present visual stories that transform the audiences, Wiley, 2010

1.3 EVERYONE "PITCHES", OR MUST LEARN TO DO IT

Due to the critical nature of the fundraising activity, pitching is one of the most important aspects that the founders of startups must learn to deal with. In some cases, there might be a person in the team who is dedicated exclusively to fundraising activities.

I remember one of my mentors in a program for acceleration in yCombinator, who, due to his successful fundraising experiences ($20.5+million raised) told me that pitching is a matter of habit and experience.

"Every situation is good for practicing," he said, then automatically pitched his startup. *"You see, Maurizio,"* Josh said, when he'd finished his pitch, *"I can't help it. It's automatic.*

You can never know how people will react to your pitch. For this reason, it's important to present it as many times as you can, to very different people, not necessarily investors, and then listen to them and study their reactions.

"You should always be ready with your best pitch, and be sure to persuade, because when the right moment comes along, it might be unexpected."

Josh was talking about all those situations when you could meet an investor: during networking sessions, during an event, an industry exhibition, or in a normal situation in the elevator. For this reason, the mentor affirmed that the best way to be ready is to be used to pitching.

Josh also stated that you can never know who is standing in front of you and what his network of contacts is. So, you should always be ready to present in the most effective way.

Don't wait for the right situation, or to be invited to the pitch competition of the year to practice your pitch.

As Guy Kawasaki says:

"Only when you know your material very well, will you be confident doing your pitch, and the only way to do this is to keep repeating it at any time. Twenty-five times is the number most people need to reach a satisfactory level. All of these pitches don't have to be addressed to investors. It could be co-founders, colleagues, family members, friends or even your dog!" [4]

[4] Kawasaki G., The art of the start, Portfolio, 2004

1.4 THE FINANCING ROUTE OF A STARTUP

Pitching is a continuous process that will involve you during the whole life cycle of your business activity.

In fact, the funds that you can receive during the life cycle of the startup aren't always the same, they change depending on the stage of the activity, the investors and the goals of the funding request.

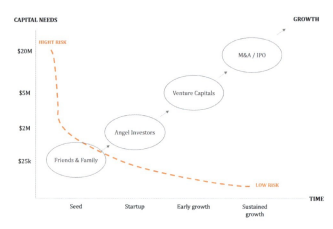

Figure 1 - The life cycle of a startup funding

FRIENDS & FAMILY

The first funding is usually raised from friends and family members. In slang, you also say *friends, family and fools,* as the latter could foolishly be willing to fund your activity, together with those who do it because they trust you and know you.

In this case, the sum raised is very low, and generally you won't need a real pitch presentation. At this stage, whoever funds you does it because they trust you, as the startup is still at its beginning. This stage is the one with the biggest risk of failure.

This type of funding, even though it's a small amount, can help you develop a first prototype, study the market, and collect the first figures based on the testing of the prototype on the target audience you identified.

Soon this information will be included in a more structured pitch presentation that you will use for the first, real funding round. [5]

In fact, you often use the funds collected during this phase to produce a professional pitch, that will turn out to be essential in the next phases.

MICRO-SEED

A small funding of $25,000-$50,000, obtained from professional investors (business angel, venture capital, incubator or business accelerator) is called a "micro-seed".

Like the preliminary funding explained in the previous paragraph, the aim is to allow founders to commit full-time to proving the value of their idea.

Usually, you work for a period of 3-6 months and at the end of this, you participate in the so-called "demo-day". The business accelerators and incubators involved will be able to help in the very first phases of the development of your business.
I advise you to really value this first conversation with people who have more experience than you. Actually, I personally

---
[5] Cremades A., The art of startup fundraising, Wiley, 2016

believe that business is not a subject that can be learnt at school or from textbooks, and certainly not at university!

Although I think that you need to read a lot in order to learn about business methods, I'm convinced that the best way to learn is through experience.

Even if the best way to get experience is to make lots of mistakes, one extra error could be fatal when you have a fledgling business that is under financed and unable to sustain itself independently. For this reason, I urge you to seriously consider any realistic acceleration or incubation opportunity on offer.

In these circumstances you will be able to get initial financing and come face to face with expert mentors (whom you should always evaluate before accepting any acceleration or incubation program) who will share their experiences and allow you to reduce mistakes, so safeguarding your startup.

SEED

This type of funding is considerably more substantial than the first two, and often comes from venture capital or angel investors. Seed funding usually ranges from around 250,000 dollars up to 1 million dollars.

This type of investment is still considered risky, so the funds which invest in these 'early stage' startups are called 'spray & pray', portfolios with many high-risk startups, many of which are destined to fail. These investment portfolios are gouged so that the startup that succeeds will compensate for all the failures.

When a startup has seed funding, it should have a product/service which is no longer a prototype, but is ready to go onto the market. So normally, at this stage, the business will also have a team which is able to deal with all the steps necessary to complete this phase.

Finally, seed funding prepares the startup for the next, more important, round of fundraising which will be substantial enough to support the business in its true form.

SERIES ROUND A

This type of financing can help your business to grow and expand into new markets. Round A financing can vary from $2million to $15million dollars.

One of the main objectives of this round is the development of chains of distribution and the consolidation of marketing strategies to increase sales. The investors expect the commercial infrastructure of the product or service to be ready for action.

Round A supports the development of new products and the access to new markets, as well the activation of business models which may seem of minor importance but are nevertheless relevant in terms of the strategic development of the business.

In this case, the investors are funds from venture capital, hedge funds, family office, private equity or business angels.

SERIES ROUND B

This round is similar to Round A, but finances businesses which show rapid growth. Investments in this round are around $7million to $10million.
At this stage, the risk is low as the business has already shown good results and is active on the market. You will be clear about your presence on the market and your ability to conquer a larger part of it, from your experience in the preceding rounds.

Round B allows you to expand your business and make it grow more rapidly than it would have, had you been financing it yourself. In real terms this means overseas expansion which often requires extra people and infrastructure to support the activity.

SERIES ROUND C

This round of funding often comes just before the IPO (initial public offering), when a company sells its shares to the public on the stock exchange for the first time.

The sums involved in this round are hard to quantify, as they range from a few million to hundreds of millions of dollars.

Apart from more rapid expansion, in this round, the business starts to consider the possibility of mergers and take-overs.

There are other rounds following round C, such as F, G etc. After round C, companies can sell their shares on the stock Exchange through an IPO.

If you want to examine some real examples, go to www.crunchbase.com where you can find a lot of valuable information about many current business situations.

For example, Snapchat had a round F funding of $1.8billion in 2016.

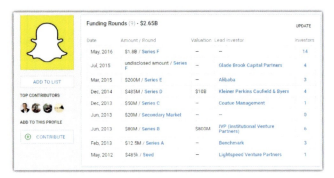

Figure 2 - Snapchat on crunchbase

Whereas Airbnb anticipated round F using ROD and private equity funds.

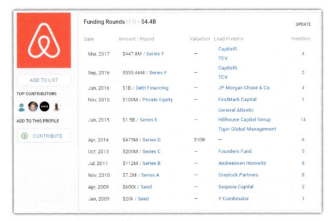

Figure 3 - Airbnb on crunchbase

IPO – INITIAL PUBLIC OFFERING

Through the IPO, the business makes its shares available to the public. Until now it had been financed by angel investors, venture capital, private equity, family office, etc. Through the quotation of shares on the stock exchange, anyone can invest in your company.

One of the reasons a business decides to go public is the necessity for rapid, extra funding for further development of the business.

Companies usually turn to the IPO when they have come to the end of the funding rounds. By this time, the business is solid and mature. Facebook, for example, went public in 2012, declaring a net income of $1billion in 2011 (+65% more than in 2010). It declared it had 845 million monthly users and 483 daily users on the 31st December 2011.

When Facebook launched its IPO in 2012, it was seen, at the time, as the most important technological IPO in the history of the United States of America. Facebook offered 421,233,615 shares at $38 a share, and earned $16 billion[6].

So now that you understand the complexity involved in financing a startup, you can see that your pitch presentation will have to evolve alongside your business. Every stage of fundraising helps you to gather the information needed to prepare for the next stage. It's an extra occasion to perfect your presentation, in readiness for the next session.

---

[6] If You Had Invested Right After Facebook's IPO (FB, TWTR), investopedia.com

1.5 MANAGING EXPECTATIONS – THE VENTURE CAPITAL FUNNEL

To embark on a startup, you must really believe in it and be ready to go against everyone and everything, including the 'syndrome of a permanent job', especially in Italy. And don't be surprised if the people closest to you don't really understand what you're doing.

Although I think it's right to motivate those who have the courage and the vocation to take this path, I often find myself in the opposite situation. In fact, many entrepreneurs nowadays are too sure of themselves and are convinced they have found the next Unicorn.

So, I decided to put a figure on the chance of a business being funded like those so called unicorns.

Premise: *a unicorn is a startup with an evaluation of over $1billion.*

CB INSIGHTS[7] studied 1098 American startups that received the first seed funding in 2008, 2009 or 2010, and then got extra funding before the 28th of February 2017.

As I already said, the financing process goes on through all your business life. It's not a question of doing a pitch, being financed and forgetting about fundraising; it's a continuous process that demands time, resources and experience.

Just think, that among the 1098 startups that received initial funding, only 46% got to the second round.

You can count Unicorns that survived this funnel on your fingers, and they are about 1% of the startups that received the first seed. To name some: Airbnb, Slack, Uber, etc.

In the last 2 years, the number of *seeds* granted to startups has grown, and this has caused a decrease of the conversion rate into unicorns.

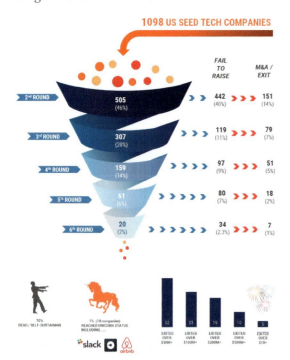

Figure 4 - The funnel of venture capital

[7] Venture capital funnel shows odds of becoming a unicorn are less than 1%, cbinsights.com

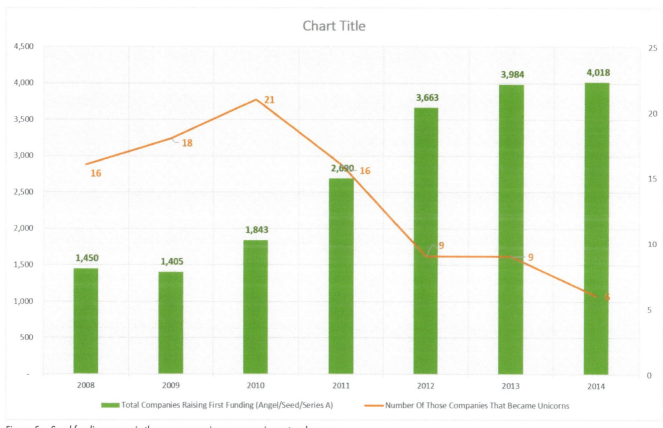

Figure 5 – Seed fundings grow in the years, so unicorn conversion rates decrease

If you're asking yourself what these famous unicorns are, here are some of the most successful names for every year mentioned below, according to the data collected from CB INSIGHTS[8].

---

[8] Your startup has a 1,28% change of becoming a unicorn, cbinsights.com

Year	Total Companies Raising First Funding (Angel/Seed/Series A)	Number Of Those Companies That Became Unicorns	Unicorn Conversion Rate	Unicorn Sample
2008	1450	16	1.10%	MongoDB, Lyft, SunRun
2009	1405	18	1.28%	Zulily, Airbnb, DataLogix
2010	1843	21	1.14%	Stripe, Slack Technologies, Funding Circle
2011	2690	16	0.59%	Warby Parker, Hortonworks, ContextLogic
2012	3663	9	0.25%	Instacart, Snapchat, Qualtrics
2013	3984	9	0.23%	Zenefits, Airwatch, Juno Therapeutics
2014	4018	6	0.15%	Magic Leap, Adyen, DJI Innovations

Figure 6 – Companies which became unicorns

At least 70% of startups stopped collecting and raising funds, but some were able to finance themselves.

However, let's be careful. Becoming self-financing and exiting the funding path can lead to reduction in growth, which, though acceptable to an entrepreneur, can never be acceptable to an investor.

So, to conclude this analysis, you should always adapt your expectations, be determined and motivated, but remember to keep your feet on the ground. The chances of your startup becoming a unicorn are similar to those of you becoming an astronaut for NASA (0.6%)[9].

---

[9] Shiro B., Insider tips on NASA's astronaut selection, astronautforhire.com

1.6 WHY SHOULD A PITCH FAIL?

There are many risks involved in such an important and delicate presentation. As I said, knowing how to present your startup is an important entrepreneurial skill that you acquire with experience. Here are some of the most common reasons for failure.

Are you ready? Pay attention, because from now on, I expect you at least to avoid the mistakes below.

1.6.1 Failure to establish an immediate connection

Each presentation is a dialogue, a connection with your audience. If you can connect to your audience, you can start a dialogue that works and transmits ideas and messages to convince them to take action.

But if we talk about an investor pitch, you must remember that for an investor, you are only one of many startups that are trying to capture their attention. I previously showed you the conversion funnel of investments, and you must have realized how difficult the job of an investor can be, having to judge thousands of pitches and identifying the few, valid investment opportunities.

This is one of the reasons why the investor will listen attentively to your investor pitch for a very brief period (as we will see later on), and why you must grab his attention from the very first slides.

I will explain the strategies for establishing an immediate connection with your audience in a later section. For the moment, keep in mind that this is something you must study really well!

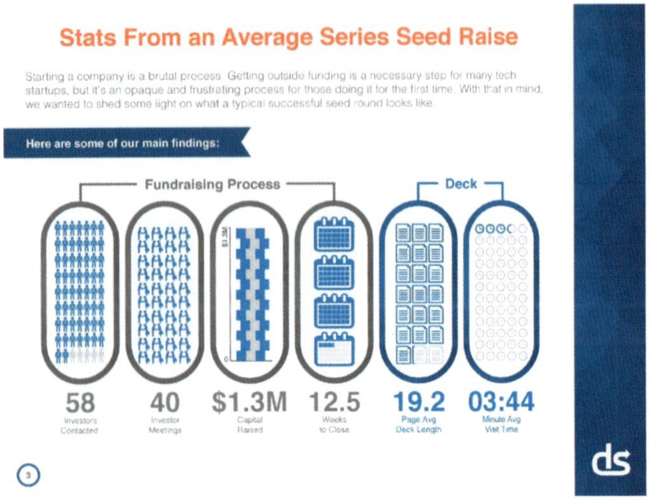

Figure 7 - Results of analysis of 200+ pitch conducted by DocSend (docsend.com)

Figure 8 - Time that investors dedicate to a pitch (docsend.com)

1.6.2 Having a badly structured pitch

A pitch is a presentation, and must have a perfect structure of contents. What we say and what we don't say makes a difference, but also the order in which we give the information and how it's structured.

DocSend manages content management and tracking solutions for digital documents. The company has analyzed over 200 pitch presentations of startups at their early stage.

The analysis has shown that investors spend on average 3.44 minutes on presentations of 19.2 pages [10].

This means that, on average, you must spend 11.8 seconds on each slide. For this reason, it's essential that:

The presentation must be structured correctly
Information must be well ordered and fluent, to avoid the investor having to skip forward or backwards to search for information.

The pitch must include essential information
The pitch must include only the information needed to catch the investors interest. Don't overload your investor pitch with unnecessary information during this initial phase, but don't leave out information that could be crucial for keeping the investor on board.

The presentation must be visually attractive (eye-catching)
The presentation must show the information at a glance. For each slide, you have 11 seconds to communicate you message to the investor, so there can't be too much text and you have to take care of the smallest details.

---

[10] What we learned from 200 startups who raised $360M, docsend.com

Carlos Espinal, partner in Seedcamp, says:

"Being over-the-top and dropping 'bombs' might get you attention, but is it the right attention? Is it focusing the attention on your message or just on yourself? Also, what about a boring slide presentation? Or a pitch that is missing product shots? [...] What happens if you say your product is simple, but then your presentation is really complicated?" [11]

Visual design for slide communication is a branch of Presentation Design
The presentation designer creates and builds layouts for slides to lead the audience through an effective and fluent experience[12].

Further on in this book I will teach you, in detail, how to build each slide in the most effective way possible.

1.6.3 Not understanding the audience

It's clear that if you're pitching to an investor that manages round C and you're looking for a micro seed, things might go wrong! Or, imagine presenting a digital startup, maybe a social network, to a group of investors interested in 3D printing.

As we will see later, understanding the audience is fundamental in defining the objectives of our communication and deciding what information we want to provide.

1.6.4 Not understanding your market

Usually the entrepreneur who knows his market earns a lot more points in the eyes of the investor. I have occasionally followed startups on acceleration programs in the biomedical sector, collaborating with strategic partners in that field.

I have seen startups introducing incredible projects, such as artificial hearts to aid in the testing of certain drugs or 3D visualization of x-rays to help surgeons during their operations, and many more.

When an entrepreneur who presents these kinds of technologies, addressed to researchers or specialized doctors, works in this field himself (as a doctor, researcher, biomedical engineer, etc.) he gains authority in the eyes of his audience.

We will see this aspect in detail, as one of the many different techniques of persuasion, but for the moment, just consider that an entrepreneur who doesn't know his market will not be credible.

Another big, but very common, mistake, is the lack of attention to Go-to-market. In fact, even though you can say you know the market, this doesn't mean you know how to get onto it with your product/service.

So, being convincing on the Go-to-market is essential if you don't want your investors to have doubts about your ability to achieve your objectives.

---

[11] 10 top fundraising fails, seedcamp.com
[12] La Cava M., Lean Presentation Design, Franco Angeli, 2017

1.6.5 Not knowing your competitors

Can you imagine your dismay if an investor stopped you during your pitch to ask you a question about a competitor that you know nothing about, whom you didn't include in your analysis?

If it happens when I'm present, I feel mortified, so I can imagine how terrible an entrepreneur must feel!

Moreover, the situation is always the same: the investor playing on his iPad during the presentations, is suddenly interested in your idea and asks himself if someone else is already doing the same thing. So, he quickly opens the browser and checks on Google.

At this point, if he finds a competitor that is not included in your presentation, he will ask about them. If you aren't there because you sent your presentation by e-mail, the investor might start doubting your capacity to analyze the situation, without being able to get an immediate answer from you.

So do an in-depth analysis of your national and international competitors and always try to be really well informed about this aspect of your business.

1.6.6 Revealing an incomplete team

Especially at the beginning, when the product doesn't exist or when you are building a prototype, the investor will judge the team.

If, during your presentation, the team looks incomplete or inadequate for the task ahead, I can tell you for sure that you will lose the attention of the investor.

We will focus on the team in a different section.

1.6.7 Revealing weak financials or an excessive request

A good business plan reveals the capacity to create a project and demonstrates the attention of the entrepreneur to the sustainability of his business.

While it might be the first time you have seen a business plan for a startup in your sector, investors see hundreds every year and often have years of experience.

If the numbers are excessive, wrong or imprecise, the investor knows immediately and you lose credibility.

The same is true for requests that are excessive or inappropriate. If you are able to raise the first €25,000-€50,000 and you present yourself with an investor pitch asking for €1 million without the numbers to support your request, you can be sure that failure is just around the corner.

1.7 Summarizing

As you might have guessed, every aspect of the pitch, from the oral presentation to the creation of each slide, both the written contents and visual information, must be managed meticulously.

Throughout this book we will focus on the most important aspects, every one of which could seriously affect the success or failure of your project.

CHAPTER 2

GET TO KNOW WHO IS IN FRONT OF YOU

Do you remember what your mum always used to say? "Do not talk to strangers".

A presentation is a moment in which you get to talk to your audience. During this "chat" you will have to convince your listeners to adopt and perhaps spread your ideas.

Convincing people you don't know is difficult, because you don't know what they'll think about your ideas.

So, if on the day of your presentation you're not prepared and you don't know who is sitting in front of you, it will be literally like talking to total strangers. You can't foresee how they will react or whether they will be at all interested in what you are talking about.

If you create a revolutionary biomedical hardware device and you apply to a business accelerator that only deals with fintech, you are bound to fail.

Do you think that knowing the profession of the people in front of you is enough to influence them? Certainly not. Audience awareness is something more profound and we are going to analyze it in depth in this chapter.

2.1 ANALYZE YOUR AUDIENCE

Before we analyse the steps of a persuasive strategy, I invite you to take a moment and think about how well you know the audience you want to persuade.

I am about to tell you a story that affected me.

Peter Coughter, the author of the book "The art of the pitch", built his agency's success: Coughter & Company, thanks to his ability to acquire important commissions by creating extremely efficient presentations.

One day, when Peter was still working for an American publicity agency, he found out that Blue Cross Blue Shield (BCBSA) – a group of insurance companies with half a million annual turnover and a secure client base of hundred millions of insured Americans - had got fed up with its New York publicity agency and wanted to change. The reason for this change was that the agency was not willing to go into the client's office and made the clients travel continuously to Washington.

As soon as he knew what had happened, Peter immediately contacted the BCBSA marketing director of that time, Ray Freson, who confirmed they were looking for a new partner in Washington D.C.

Peter promptly says: "We are the perfect partner for you here in Richmond, Virginia, we are just down the road!"
In fact, it was 180-190 km away.

Figure 1 - From Washington D.C. to Richmond, Virginia.

Ray said that, because of their previous negative experience, they were looking for someone who was in Washington D.C. and even a two-hour drive would have been a problem.
At that point, Peter said that the distance would be his problem, and he would do all the traveling himself, but Ray still wouldn't listen.

For that reason, Peter, put in a difficult position, started talking about successful projects he'd completed with clients in Washington D.C.

Ray, who knew about all the most successful projects in his area, began to show interest.

He said he would try to convince the four board members to invite Peter's agency to the pitch.

The agency for which Peter worked was then invited to the pitch. Peter knew that, thanks to their ability in creating efficient presentations, they would have a good chance of success.

However, their agency was the only one out of town, and as if that wasn't enough, the 4 board members wanted the presentation to be held in the office of the different agencies.

Therefore the 4 bosses would have had to go to Richmond but they would not have been happy at all.

The contract was withdrawn, but the target was still far off, and the journey was long.
Peter asked Ray to send him as much information as he could about the 4 board members.
Ray, who supported Peter's agency, provided him with complete biographies of the 4 bosses, complete with photos so that Peter would be able to identify them all.

After careful analysis, Peter discovered that the 4 had something in common. In fact, 3 of them had been in the army, and the other was one was passionately interested in military culture.

At that time Peter and his colleagues were reading Sun Tzu's famous book: "The art of war", a book that still today has a lot to teach us about to modern strategy.
If you haven't read it yet, I recommend it.

For this reason, he decided to base the presentation of the agency's successful cases related to clients in Washington D.C., by creating links with the principles illustrated by Sun Tzu. Each case was going to be presented as if it were a real military operation.

Obviously, each operation would serve to illustrate a solution to the clients' specific needs.

Mentioning Peter:

"Remember that even when you have to talk about yourself, you always have to talk about the client".

Everything seemed ready but, since the day of the presentation would mean the clients had to travel 200km, and knowing that distance was the reason for the break with their old agency, all of this was not enough.

Peter knew that it was necessary to find a way to attract the audience's attention from the beginning and keep it until the moment in which they said "yes" or they would have stopped the presentation.

And so, the decisive day arrived. The 4 entered the room and were visibly irritated. First of all, Peter and his team greeted them personally (thanks to the pictures they had received). After they sat down, Peter started his presentation.

Peter: *"Do you know what my favorite film is? It's Conan the Barbarian. My favorite scene is when Conan is sent to the general's party. On that occasion, the general addresses his son, sits in front of Conan, and asks him which is the best feeling in the world. The son is sure that it is the feeling of the wind in his hair while he is riding his steed through the steppe.*

The general, not content with his son's answer, asks him the same question again. The son, knowing that he had to change his answer, said that the best emotion he had ever felt was defeating his enemies and hearing their wives' moans."

At this point Peter takes a break, waits for the audience's reaction and starts again saying *"And this is what advertising is for us! This is the reason why today's presentation is called: 'The art of war' "*.

On hearing these words one of the 4 bosses started to applaud. The audience was won over and listened carefully to the entire presentation.

At the end the bosses said that they still had to visit another agency, but they were so struck by the presentation, that they eventually decided to work with Peter's agency.

I told you this story because I find it a brilliant example of how knowing your audience can transform a battle that seemed lost before it began, into a crushing victory.

This story inspired me and has influenced my way of studying the audience before each of my presentations, therefore I hope that from now on it can inspire you.

2.1.1 Your audience is the hero

I remember one day I was involved in a pitch competition for startups whom I had helped to create their investor pitches.

On that occasion, at a certain point, "famous" entrepreneurs (those who had made it) were due to speak.

Everyone was waiting for their presentations, since these businessmen represented the point of arrival, or maybe just an important goal for those who would win the competition that day and who aimed to grow and create a solid and sustainable business. So, these entrepreneurs should have been the idols of the start-ups that were taking part in the competition that day.

The first of the two speakers left me speechless!
This man stood on stage and started talking about how successful he had been in his entrepreneurial activity. Slides about his best clients, interviews and articles on his business, collaborations with famous universities, his international resonance and other fantastic things, started to scroll through.

This person talked for about half an hour without ever saying what he actually did.

I could hear a small voice (see Kawasaki G., "The art of start") inside of me that kept asking: "What does this man do?"

Suddenly, towards the middle of the presentation there was a video, and I thought it was a technique of public speaking or of audience engagement that builds curiosity and then it reveals all the answers with the classic, striking video. However, the video showed the same things he had already said, including his fantastic TV and radio interviews that, this time, we could see 'live'.

When the presentation was finished, he thanked the audience and closed his presentation saying "stay angry stay foolish", quoting good old Steve Jobs.

Believe me, I was left speechless; his presentation had certainly illustrated his own skills but he never spoke about what he really did.

This often happens to me, when I find myself working on presentations in the field of management consulting. Usually a client believes he needs a consulting project; therefore the so called consulting firms create a pitch presentation in order to win the project.

Have you ever had the opportunity to see one?

They are usually all the same, both in terms of content and, even worse, in terms of structure. They are full of recurrent messages like: we are the market leaders, we are the best consultants of the year, we are absolutely the strongest in this field, we are operative all around the world, we have been working in this market for a year now, we are.

This continuous praise about themselves gets so radical that the presentations sent by the competitors are all the same. Therefore, they are all market leaders, and best consultants of the year.

Who is the winner? Those who remain silent and really listen to the client. In this arena which seems to be a competition where the winner is the one who screams the loudest, the most intelligent way to make a difference is to start the presentation by talking about the client, instead of talking about ourselves.

There will always be time to show your skills and qualifications that can help to solve your client's problems, but first you have to convince the client that you understood the problem itself and you know what to work on.

Anyway remember that, during your presentation, you are not the hero, but your audience is. The role that best suits you, being a supervisor, is that of the coach.

G. Reynolds (author of presentation Zen) says that if the audience was Luke Skywalker, you would be master Yoda. Using a film as an example again, I could say that if your audience was Daniel-san, you would be master Myagi.

You have the task to guide your audience in its business, but it will always be the people that follow you, who have to face the change.

You present the pitch but the investors are the one to decide whether to experience this with you and support you in your growth.

2.1.2 People act in a selfish way

If Apple had launched a new computer saying: "We create the best computers on the market, because they are easy to use and nice to look at", would you have bought it?
It is not interesting and it is not how Apple usually communicates, right?

Let's try this way: "In everything we do we believe in fighting the status quo, we believe in an innovative and different approach.
We initiate change and fight the status quo, caring about our products' design and making them affordable for everyone. That is why we build the best computers on the market".

Would you buy it now? Let's say there are more chances that this second sentence inspired you the most.

Thus, in his famous speech at TEDx, Simon Sinek[1] explains how people tend to react when they believe in your same values. In other words, Sinek says that people buy the "why" and not the "what".

If you think about it, Apple is none other than a computer producer, like any other of its competitors. Dell, for example, produces mp3, but if you had to choose between an mp3 Dell and an IPod, you would not give it a second thought. Why? Because even though technically they are both mp3s, you are not buying a music player but the world that it represents and the reason why it was created.

This is why you feel comfortable buying Apple Smartphones, iPods, computer and much more. Not because they are the best on the market, but to show that you believe in the same values as Apple. You do it for yourself, not for others.

---

[1] Sinek S., How great leaders inspire action, ted.com

People act in a selfish way, according to what they like to show. Sinek explains why 25,0000 people showed up without an invite, at the right time, under the August sun to Martin Luther King's famous Speech. Because they believed in what King believed in, and they wanted to show it to others. No one that day was in the square for King, but for themselves.

Sinek talks about the golden circle (see figure 2), a model that represents what stands at the base of human behavior. If you want to persuade the audience you will have to be able to communicate the reasons that brought you to do something. So you have to start from the center of the circle and move towards the outside.

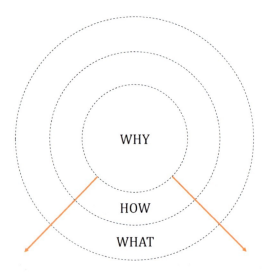

Figure 2 - Golden Circle Simon Sinek

Briefly, people that are able to communicate the reasons for their actions are more influential and tend to be followed more readily.

2.1.3 What are investors looking for?

The investor thinks in terms of profit: if he finances a start-up, he expects a return on his investment with a reasonable re-entry time.

The riskier the investment, the more its potential return will be. Start-ups are a very risky investment, because, as we saw, one in ten succeeds and the other nine disappear.

Therefore, the investors, in order to build a fruitful business, have to know that if they invest in ten start-ups, each one of them has to guarantee the potential to pay back the entire portfolio and also earn from it.

Ideally an investor seeks the perfect investment: low risk and high efficiency. Therefore during the pitch he will be interested in each piece of information that will permit him to guarantee these two points.

An important, existing problem for a specific audience means that the activity has reasons to exist and it can obtain a positive outcome. A solution that really helps in solving a problem also justifies the company's existence.

A strong team with the right skills and experiences that permit it to implement your project, allows you think that there are more chances of success.

Again, a traction or tests that support the product-solution fit (Steve blank, the four steps to the epiphany) ensure that the investor is in faced with a product that has the right to exist because someone is interested in it.

You've probably understood that factors like: problem, solution, team, traction, or test results are the most important in order to reduce an investor's potential risk.

Conversely, a rich and interesting market in which it is able to develop a strong business model with clear distinguishing points in respect to current incumbent or competitor, indicates a return on the investment worthy of attention.

Investors do not only invest their money, they also invest their time.

Therefore, they want to be sure they are investing their resources with the best people.

The investors may want an active part in the business management and they could become important stakeholders.

This is the reason why choosing the right team to work with is fundamental for an investor. Usually a team is chosen in relation to its skills and experiences in project implementation.

In reality the active investor knows he will spend a lot of time with the team he is going to finance, and this is also something that is going to influence the investor's choice. Indeed, the investors want to be part of a team they like, that convinces them of its strength, and with which it is interesting to work.

Finally, you have to consider that not all investors are the same. As you saw in the first chapter, different investors intervene in several phases of the financial journey of a startup.

For example, an investment fund will look for a start-up with a strong product, patented technology and a fruitful and graduated business. Its target is clearly profit, but it is also interested in the management of its investment portfolio.

A business angel on the other hand, may also decide to invest only because he is passionate about the idea, or he personally feels the problem and he believes that the team could solve it. Therefore, it might seem that the business angel is trying to confirm the strength of the team and its ability to develop more than one solution for this problem.

Obviously, even a BA invests in something to earn money from, but, in respect to a VC, other personal reasons can apply.

During one of my past entrepreneurial experiences, I dealt with marketing and start-up business development. I was looking for an important industrial partnership, and, after a few attempts, thanks to Linkedin, I was able to get an appointment with a group director.

We presented the idea, showing the benefits of a potential collaboration and we immediately gained his support. Our interlocutor was willing to help us but at the same time he explained how complicated and extremely bureaucratic corporate dynamics were.

At first we were a bit confused, we could not understand whether he wanted to help us or not, but in the end he said he was interested in investing in the idea himself.

At the time, we did not have a solid business model and we had certainly not presented it highlighting the investment benefits.

However, that same day that person fell in love with the idea because he personally felt involved in the problem we were trying to solve. Most probably he was not sure whether our solution was the best one, but he wanted to help us in our future growth and he certainly liked our team and our approach.

So why is it important to acknowledge the differences in potential investors' interests?

Because these small details can make a difference if used in the presentation of your pitch.

As you will see in the next chapters, these differences will help you define the pitch structure and which sections it is best to invest time and resources in during the presentation.

2.2 THE FIRST IMPRESSION IS WHAT REALLY COUNTS

Since I work in the world of start-ups, it often happens that I have to sign NDAs (non disclosure agreement) before the entrepreneur trusts me enough to tell me about his latest idea, that could change the world.

The entrepreneur usually explains how unique his idea is, that he is sure that no one in the world has ever thought of it, that the entrepreneurial activity's success is based on being the first one on the market.

My expectations grow fast and each time I hope to be the one chosen to see a new light. So I always sign without hesitation and wait for the material.

But when I receive the documents, I am surprised by the fact that this idea is not brilliant, but rather, old, already tested and rejected, or maybe the team has no experience, skills or any hope of bringing it onto the market.

How many times do you see unsustainable ideas? I remember an investor saying: "In our country we are not missing resources to finance start-ups, but start-ups in which to invest". I would also add that we are missing start-ups able to attract investment.

To have a brilliant idea is not that easy. However, in doing business, it is not the hardest thing. Knowing how to sell your idea, in order to bring it onto the market, involve employees or gather investments is definitely more difficult.

But why is it so hard knowing how to sell your own idea? Were you ever so sure about the value of your idea that you thought your audience did not truly understand its true potential?

The truth is that in many cases, from the moment your audience has laid eyes on you, your presentation will fail after the first 150 milliseconds.[2]

In 1970 psychologists N. Cantor and W. Mischel from Standford University stated that humans use predefined stereotypes to categorize a stranger when they are approached for the first time.

Investors, more than anyone else in the business world, have to filter many investment ideas. It would be impossible to accurately judge them all, therefore they unconsciously resort to stereotypes.

In other words, each of us has certain stereotypes in mind that develop from previous knowledge or past experiences.

Do you ever find yourself sitting in a waiting room looking at people passing by and wondering about their lives? You could think about their profession, their values and their names. I am sure that most of the time you would have an answer, which you feel quite sure about.

This is just an example of how easily we tag strangers in order to identify and classify them.

We do not like what we do not know, and it is easier to control it if we consider it as a part of something we already know and which we are able to deal with.

Therefore, the easiest way for an investor to judge an idea, is to judge the person who presents it to him.
Since negative comments are more memorable than positive ones, a good pitch can be destroyed in a few moments.

---

[2] Elsbach K.D., How to pitch a brilliant idea, Harvard Business Review

Kimberly Elsbach from the University of California identifies four negative stereotypes that you can fall into:

2.2.1 Pushover

Figure 3 - Pushover: a person easy to influence

Someone that abandons an idea rather than defending it. I remember a start-up pitch in the Internet field, who did not know how to cash in on his business, so he presented 6 potential business models.

During the presentation, one investor expressed doubts about some of them and gave his reasons.

The entrepreneur, without hesitation, immediately excluded these models and tried to sell the others.

You must realise, that in this situation the individual immediately loses his credibility and will find it impossible to sell anything.

One of my bosses once said: "Leadership means having a point of view and sticking to it, whether it's right or wrong". Investors want to finance leaders who are able to change the world, not those who don't even have a vision about how to cash in on their business activities.

2.2.2 Robot

Figure 4 - The robot presents "rapid-fire"

The classic "rapid-fire" presentation. Presenting the pitch all in one breath, following slide after slide of the speech prepared.

The worst thing happens when you reply to people's questions with clearly prepared and memorized answers. I'm not saying that preparing for possible questions that the investors could ask is a bad idea, but in some cases, the answer is not the right one to that question, only the closest chosen from the ones prepared previously.
The speaker then loses credibility, as it seems he's acting the part prepared for the investors and has no real capacity for managing a business.

A good entrepreneur knows his business and how to present it in the best way. A presentation learnt off by heart makes the entrepreneur look unprepared and insecure. Who would invest in someone who doesn't know his own business?

2.2.3 Second hand car salesman

Figure 5 - The seller doesn't listen

The speakers go on with their speech, completely ignoring input along their path.

Some presenters don't answer questions and carry on with their presentation, trying to sell their project.

However, a dialogue is based on listening; it makes a conversation more human. What kind of dialogue is it if you're the only one who's speaking?

I happened to meet an entrepreneur, who regardless of what was happening during the pitch, would go on with his presentation. If someone had a question he would listen to it and then go on, without replying.

This kind of attitude can make people think you are arrogant and pretentious and no one would want to work in your team.

Normally investors want to have a conversation with you and they want to feel involved in the project.

C. Lipp, famous pitch coach at Standford University, talks about the first time he made a pitch for Paul Graham (yCombinator)[3].

Lipp says he was perfectly prepared for the meeting, his speech was ready and he had a beautiful presentation. As an expert public speaker, he had the experience to prepare and manage an important presentation.

Nevertheless, when he started his pitch, P. Graham interrupted him and asked him an unexpected and difficult question and then another question followed and another one, until the time available for his presentation ended. Lipp didn't end his presentation and didn't reply properly to all the unexpected questions so he wasn't selected and his startup couldn't be part of the program.

This accident can teach us how important it is to know our audience and the way people behave, but most of all that people are naturally prone to converse. So, we must create a dialogue with our audience and present by creating a conversation, not by giving it a list of pre-packed information.

[3] Lipp C., The startup pitch, 2014

2.2.4 Beggar

Figure 6 – The beggar begs the audience

The kind of attitude to avoid is that of the presenter who has realized he hasn't engaged the audience and hasn't involved people, and starts begging.

It might seem incredible! But I really happened to hear speakers say: *"We really need your funding otherwise we risk failure"*.

No investor wants to fund entrepreneurs who beg. So how can we avoid being labeled?

The first step is to knowing what dangerous stereotypes that could be assigned to you. You must absolutely avoid the 4 we talked about, otherwise your pitch will fail.

Furthermore, during her research Doctor Elsbach explains some behavior common to all successful pitchers: the ability to actively involve the audience.

Doctor Elsbach talks about a very young writer who has just returned from Japan and presents a new idea for a TV show to a television network.

The idea is to tell the story of a young guy who goes to Japan and learns how to play taiko drums.

Figure 7 – Japanese taiko drums

The guy is very young and lacks experience. He is really involved and passionate about his idea but he has never created a show before and isn't very good at presenting.

Suddenly he asks someone from the staff to help him with special shots. While the cameraman tries the most absurd positions to create spectacular shots, the young guy shows particular positions to play the drums.

Very soon the show becomes a collaboration between the young man and the production team. Everyone works together to make the show special.

So the attention moves from a cold analysis and a precise choice (yes or no) to a process of cooperation where whoever judges is actively involved.

The technique of the active participation of the audience is a good method during a meeting if you're alone with potential investors. In this case, you have time to actively involve people in your project.

During a pitch competition, because of little time, pressure and the vast audience, it's difficult to involve investors, but this technique could be useful when people start asking questions at the end of the speech or during the presentation.

Keep in mind that it's very important to manage the presentation like a conversation with the audience.

2.3 CATCH ATTENTION

The most common mistake entrepreneurs make is believing that a 60 minutes meeting with the investor means having attention his for 60 minutes: actually there will be a loss of attention in the first 5 minutes [4].

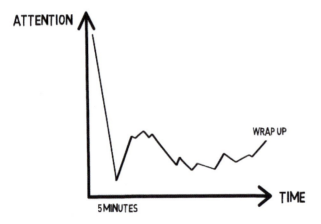

Figure 8 - loss of attention happens in the first 5 minutes

In my own experience, if investors have seen one pitch after another all day long, these 5 minutes are very generous, because investors will feel tired and will have a much quicker loss of attention.

Imagine what happens if you lose the attention of investors in the initial phases. It will be very difficult for you to convince them to invest in your product if they haven't listened to its presentation.

So if you want to win over your audience, you must do it right from the beginning of the presentation.

So to start, introduce yourself to the audience with an open minded and friendly attitude. There's nothing worse than a speaker who introduces himself talking about his references which prove he's qualified enough to talk about his topic.

This is trying to stress the attention of the audience. R. Cialdini talks about reciprocation; this principle states that people feel obliged towards those who give them something free of charge.

During a presentation you can share a personal story with the audience, an experience or something you learnt, and you can do it without asking for something in exchange.

Don't portray yourself as a sales person, but as a mentor; show that you're interested in people's problems and don't try to sell them something.

STORYTELLING

Figure 9 - Stories have always been a powerful method to involve and excite

[4] Hilaly A., How to present to investors, sequoiacap.com

One of the oldest and most well-known techniques in the world and still the best hooking technique we talk about for its effectiveness, it to start with a story.

A story can show the audience you are human like everyone else, you are touchable. When you tell a story you show you have feelings and can be touched, so it will be easier to create an emotional connection between yourself and the audience. The audience will feel closer to you and will trust you and if people start trusting you, you will earn their attention!

As we have seen, when you start talking, you won't always be the first startup to be introduced and investors will be tired after other presentations. Bad presentations will wear out investors and if you're not among the first speakers you will suffer the consequences.

For this reason, when you start, people are not all ready for your call to action and if you think of asking for funding right from the beginning, you will be sure to fail.
Instead, if you start with a story, the beginning of your presentation will be easier to follow and if the tale is captivating, the audience will be attracted by your words.

To make a story interesting and captivating they must feel they're living the story. This is why knowing your audience and every kind of person in front of you is essential. The better you know your audience the easier it will be to tell a story that people can feel part of.

Peter Coughter says:

"People love to hear stories about themselves, they want to feel they're living your story. The better you know the audience the easier it will be to talk to them. I don't want to know if they are a Marketing Director or Brand Manager, but I want to know what they studied, if they have hobbies, if they have a family, children and if the latter are sons or daughters. Once I know them I will be able to tell a story than can involve them". [5]

Start the pitch explaining the problem with a story in which investors can feel involved, something that feels close to them. If the correlation between the audience and your story isn't clear, explain why people should be directly or indirectly involved in your story.

If you have no real tale to talk about, make it up and be believable. During this phase of the presentation you need to engage the audience and avoid loss of attention, so don't hesitate!

The important thing is that your story, the analogy, or metaphor that you talk about must be related to you presentation. With a story you can explain the context before talking about the problem/solution. You can think of the story as a catwalk that leads the audience from an initial moment of indifference, to listen to the problem and then be interested in knowing the solution.

If you create the context, the main character and the moment, and manage to engage the audience, you will notice that people suffer when you explain the problem and will want to know how to solve it.

[5] coughter.com

As an example I will talk about the famous Ted Talk by Jeorge Soto - The Future of Early Cancer Detection:

Figure 10 - Jorge Soto – The Future of Early Cancer Detection

"More or less one year ago my aunt started suffering from a bad back and went to the doctor. She was told the pain was due to the fact she had been playing tennis for almost 30 years. They recommended some therapy, but after a while she didn't feel better, so the doctors did more tests."

Jorge was describing the context and introducing the main character of the story.

"The X-ray exams showed she had a lung injury so doctors thought it was a strain in the muscles and tendons of the spine, but after a couple of weeks of therapy it didn't get better."

The main character bumps into the first problem and starts his adventure.

"The doctors decided to do a biopsy and two weeks later, they got the results. It was phase 3 lung cancer. Her lifestyle was healthy, she never smoked, never drank alcohol and played sport for half her life."

We got to the most important part of the introduction, the moment when Jeorge explains the correlation between his story and the audience sitting in front of him:

"Maybe this is why it took them such a long time to make the correct diagnosis. Most of you might, unfortunately, be familiar with this story."

Jeorge is creating a first indirect relationship between the audience and his story and is inviting people to think about someone close to them who lived through a similar situation. Jeorge also knows he can be even more incisive and he creates a direct strong correlation:

"One person out of three sitting among the audience will be diagnosed with this kind of cancer, and one out of 4 will die from it."

Jeorge focused on fear, to scare the audience and get their attention.

And now that he has engaged his audience Jeorge can introduce the problem that he will talk about in his presentation:

"The diagnosis of a cancer changed the life of my family but also the continuous going back and forward for new tests, with different doctors, explaining the symptoms and rejecting one disease after another was stressful and frustrating, especially for my aunt. This is what the diagnosis of cancer meant for us right from the beginning of this story." [6]

Don't you want to know how the story ends?

Jeorge seduced the audience by introducing a presentation with a personal story that is also the story of everyone else.

---

[6] The Future of Early Cancer Detection? | Jorge Soto | TED Talks, youtube.com

Everyone is interested in the problem and automatically everyone wants to know the solution.

As Pixar's storytellers say, what makes a story interesting and exciting is the ability of the speaker to transmit his feeling to the audience. There is only one way to make this happen: the story must be personal, touching and close to the speaker.

If you tell a story in which you were personally involved, you are naturally driven to transmit the emotions and sensations that you felt.

Those emotions will engage the audience, if you will be good enough to make them feel your story is their story.

So to win over the audience from the first phases of the presentation, build a story that will touch you personally, live the story when you talk about it and make sure your investors are living I too. Use the introduction to get maximum attention and present the problem.

2.4 LEARN HOW TO MANAGE INTERACTIONS

If the investors want to feel part of the team and take part in the discussion and if you managed to create proper conversation dynamics with the audience, you will soon be asked the questions you fear so much.

First of all, stay calm, asking questions is normal. Investors don't ask questions because they're mean but because they're interested and want to know more.

Figure 11 - Don't be afraid of investor's questions

I want to tell you a tale about my childhood.

When I was very young I enjoyed playing basketball, I wasn't very good and my coach kept telling me off and shouting at me every time I did something wrong. Every time, I felt bad and I was literally terrified of making a mistake.

Once he told me off so severely I didn't want to play anymore, so he came close to me and said: "Remember you shouldn't worry when I shout at you, you will have to worry if I stop doing it".

So if you are pressurized by an investor, it means he's interested in your project and if he insists, it means he really wants an answer. The more he asks, the more he proves he's interested in your idea.

In addition to all of this, there is the passing fad whereby pitch competitions are good if investors on stage are cruel and destroy the entrepreneurs. So they might ask questions aggressively.

Questions are part of every presentation if the audience is barely interested in your ideas, so calm down, read the following lines and answer calmly.

Look at the pitches that won the techrunch disrupt and you will see that they all leave some time for questions at the end of the speech. Nobody hopes the investors will forget, it's highly desirable that they ask as many questions as they can! If you are asked many questions, don't be on the defensive. I've seen entrepreneurs that went against the investors questions to defend their point of view.

An investor might make a correct observation that shows the weaknesses of your speech or your business, but this doesn't mean you must deny the investor the right to question you during a competition, just to prove that you're right.

Investors see pitches every day, are active in the startup environment and have often been entrepreneurs themselves before you. So if they spot a weakness, it means they're the person you want in your team.

If they know the problem, they could even have a solution for you and by focusing your attention on a certain point, they are trying to understand if their experience can add value to your team.

During the conversation, take advantage of their experience, identify your weakness, explain the reasons if there are any, and if you know them, and then ask them to help you by checking if they have an answer.

Remember you should always take on responsibility for any the wrong choices that have damaged your business. If you made the wrong decision in the past and this led to mistakes being made, at least you are protecting your leadership.

It's better to have a leader that makes mistakes rather that a non-leader to rule the company.

So get to know your responsibilities and be conscious of the issues. Blame yourself and say how you want to solve the problems.

Finally, another essential matter, you must always be honest. I remember when my boss and I were conducting a job interview to take on a new person in the company. He was sitting in front of us and we had his CV. Among his interests he expressed a profound passion for wine.

My boss is passionate about wine himself and to make the candidate feel relaxed, started to talk about wine, but the candidate started to panic and could hardly follow the discussion.

We found out that he wasn't really passionate about wine, but the values and significance of this sector seemed close to the ones of our company so he added this lie.

The problem was that, at this point, we couldn't trust him anymore and we started to have doubts about every other section of his CV.

I am saying this to make you understand that trust in speaker is essential in every conversation.
The famous investor David Rose says that the most important value he looks for in entrepreneurs is integrity. Investors don't fund someone who they do not trust.

Are you not completely sure about this? Do you still think that maybe you can really benefit from a "little" lie?

I will talk about the time when my co-founder was presenting our startup to a pitch-competition. After a while someone asked something that questioned the existence of our whole project and threatened to undermine the real utility of the service we were developing.

My co-founder was not a marketing guy but he managed technical aspects so he decided to lie by making up the numbers of searches acquired from keywords analysis on Google.

The investor who was skeptical, asked us to open Google Ad words and show those numbers immediately, and my partner had to tell the truth.

In that moment, our pitch lost credibility and we lost the competition.

If you don't know the answer, say it, take note and say you will work hard and focus on it deeply. Don't be afraid of admitting you don't know the answer as it's an act of responsibility that will earn you the trust of the audience.

> **C. Lipp says:**
>
> *"Dialogue is a dance between reaching your goals and the satisfaction of the investors' desires"* [7]

[7] Lipp C., The startup pitch, 2014

During your presentation you might be interrupted by a question that anticipates topics you haven't talked about yet, for example if you're talking about the issue and someone asks you a question about the team.

This happens because investors may already know the problem or might already know what you are talking about, so to go straight to the point, they want the information they need to judge the project.

Generally speaking, I suggest always considering the question people ask, but remember to follow the structure of the pitch.

In the next chapter, we will develop the best structure to build a pitch, the sequence of subjects that gives value to your presentation and that you must never change.

Never allow your investors to dominate your presentation with their questions. If someone has a question that is not related to what you're talking about, be sure you have understood the question and say you will answer later on when you're discussing that topic.

A very useful technique to show you've understood the question and at the same time give the audience value is to repeat the question, for those who haven't understood. This way you are showing respect to everyone and you are sure you've understood the question properly.

You must manage the conversation with your audience with respect, be open to useful criticism and always be ready to question yourself.

2.5 Summarizing

Knowing you audience in depth needs preparation and study but is essential if you want your audience to trust you.

If people trust you, you will have their attention and you will be in the best situation to present your startup effectively.

Be honest and helpful, but respected, don't let investors control the presentation. Remember the audience is your hero but you are their mentor, so don't let the roles get swapped.

3
CHAPTER

HOW TO PERSUADE THE AUDIENCE

The pitch is a presentation, and the presentation's purpose is to convince the audience to do something it might not otherwise do.

Presentations, unlike every other form of communication, give you the unique chance to get in touch with the audience and establish a deep connection with them. To be on a stage and talk in person, with slides that support you - it's the best way to awaken the concern of the audience towards your project.

Think about it for a moment. What is a pitch, after all? A pitch is exactly a presentation, with a defined audience and a purpose, often similar to the need of raising finances for a start-up project.

But how to use slides in order to be so persuasive as to convince someone to finance your project?

3.1 PERSUASION TECHNIQUES

We have seen with Simon Sinek that people act in function of "why", and not "what". Nobody likes to be told what to do. People want to know why they should do something.

To convince someone to do something they would do differently requires the skill of persuasion.

Do you feel able to convince someone?

An effective presentation is a dialogue, a negotiation and a learning process in real time, during which the conductor leads the audience to adopt their point of view.

Persuasion requires the understanding of the alternative point of view and the awareness of the audience. Moreover, a presentation is where the arguments are brought to the attention of the public in a lively way, sustained with data and experiences.

During the presentation, the most skilled conductors are able to establish an emotive connection with the audience and create a preferential communication channel for their messages.

To be able to convince means also being able to listen and comprehend the needs of your audience. A good persuader is able to accept compromises and take into consideration the others' needs in the final solution.

The persuasion techniques is covered in many other books. We will take the cue from the most consolidated principles in order to build a powerful model, easy to apply for your next investor pitch presentation.

3.2 PRACTICAL GUIDE TO PERSUASION

According to the results of the research[1], there are three fundamental principles at the bottom of a persuasive presentation:

1. Credibility
2. Focus on the audience
3. Emotionality

The skillful and combined use of these principles is crucial to achieve a successful investor pitch.

3.2.1 Credibility

Example – if a stranger asked you to finance a project you've never heard about, would you finance it?

What if your best friend asked you to finance his spaceship, in order for him to travel to Mars. Would you finance him? Unless your friend has experience as a spaceship engineer, you would probably not become his principal sponsor.

According to Jay A. Conger, Professor of Organizational Behaviors at the University of Southern California's Marshall School of Business, a person's credibility is built on two principal factors:

1. Knowledge of the subject
2. His connections

Basically, someone knows what they're talking about because they either have previous knowledge of the subject, or they know someone who does. He would be more credible than someone who has no experience at all in it.

If Mark Zuckerberg asked for funding to launch a new social network that could change the world, he wouldn't have a problem in finding sponsors.

Experience is the reason why, in cultures different from ours, failure is seen as a critical factor of success for an entrepreneur.

I can tell you that the best mentors that I have encountered during my entrepreneurial path were always those who had already gone through the problems that I was trying to solve. It was never interesting for me to talk with the mentor who had the most pretentious business position.

When I am searching out things to learn, I search out people who have experienced the frustration of not being able to solve the problems I faced – or, at least tried to solve them! If someone has failed before, however, it does not mean that they can't make a good business. Entrepreneurship is not learned through books, and there is no other way to learn it than through practical experience. I believe that failure can lead to great wisdom.

Credibility and experience go hand in hand. Aristotle was speaking about ethos - the speaker's credibility to the audience, thanks to his authority and knowledge of the subject. For example, if you have a presentation for building a house, it's going to seem a lot more credible coming from an architect than from a doctor.

An entrepreneur that has already done business in the field concerned, would be more useful to your project as a mentor than a manager who has never tried the entrepreneurial dimension.

For you, it you will achieve more credibility when utilizing someone with experience. In the same way, when you disclose your start-up, you will be more credible if you have experience in the field where you are going to do business. The other thing that lends credibility for someone is their links to their networks of social connections. If you negotiate

---

[1] Cialdini R., The Psychology of Persuasion, Haperbusiness, 2006; Conger J.A., The Necessary Art of Persuasion, Harvard Business Review

with someone that you know and trust, he will automatically seem credible to you. Think of the initial financial rounds supported by friends and relatives.

Why would they finance you? Because they trust you, because they know you as a reliable person, and because they believe you are doing things in the best possible way. Indeed, research demonstrates that people known as reliable and honest make less effort in persuading others. This happens because people invest in whom they trust.

R. Cialdini says that people prefer to answer positively to others they know or like. Therefore, we say yes more easily to people we like, that attract us physically, or that we consider similar to us.

Sometimes, Cialdini says, by simply having the name of the person you are selling to, something can improve our persuasion chances.

Has it happened that someone asks where you are from and suddenly, when both of you discover to be from the same place, a positive confidence is built between both of you? If you think about it, maybe you don't know that person, but the simple fact that you have something in common makes you think that you play for the same team.

In this case, credibility can have a viral effect. For example, if investors finance you because they trust you, there may be other investors in their network willing to invest in you because they trust the people who believe in you. Therefore, trust can flow in networks on many levels.

At this point, if more people invest in you, others might be encouraged to know more about it, or maybe take part directly only because others do it. This is an example of social confirmation (social proof – Cialdini R., The Psychology of Persuasion).

If you can already attract investments, you can benefit from what marketers refer to as the "halo effect".

If a person is good at doing something, then he will be able to do many other things, and vice versa. If we make a snap judgment that he is not able to do something, then, as far as we're concerned, he is not able to do anything.[2]

Phil Rosenzweig, author of "The Halo Effect", says:

"Much of our belief about business performance is influenced by the halo effect [...] when a firm is growing and produces income, we tend to think that it has a brilliant strategy, a visionary CEO, motivated people and a vibrant culture. When performance vanishes, we are prone to say that the strategy was wrong, the CEO became arrogant, people are unsatisfied, and the culture is wrong".

In all its simplicity, the halo effect says that if you are brilliant in something, then you are seen brilliant in all the other things. The same is valid for the negative.

Consequently, we could think that, if you are someone who already has success among the investors, you will probably be able to handle the business as well.
This is the reason why it's fashionable among digital marketers to post their photos with their Ferrari, busy with incredible parties on the beach, or spectacular overseas travels. Attempts are being made to make the audience think that if you are rich, then you are really good at your job. This representation reinforces your credibility to the audience and lays the foundations for a successful fundraising campaign.

[2] The halo effect, economist.com

If I have no experience in the industry and I don't have the right connections, how can I be credible in the eyes of investors?

Suppose you don't have the crucial knowledge in your network that you need to project credibility, and that you are too young to have the required experience in order to convince investors of your abilities. How can you earn that grain of credibility to be taken seriously?

According to Jay A. Conger, there are a few different possible alternatives.

You could learn as much as you can about the subject, using digital channels, and you surely know that you can learn everything on Internet nowadays. Or you can attend a school course, completing a master's degree, reading books, and so on.

However, this method could take a lot of time, and time is a resource that is not on your side. If you are busy putting your heart and soul into a start-up, the last thing you want to do is dedicate yourself to a master's degree in an effort to sell your business.

Alternatively, you could hire an expert on the subject to side with you and sustain your point of view. In that case, if the guru says so, he will surely be more credible than you, and you could take advantage of his credibility to persuade the audience.

R. Cialdini, Professor of Psychology at the Arizona State University, affirms that people respect authority and are prone to adopt experts' opinions. When people are hesitant, they look around for someone who knows more about the subject.

In our everyday life, we all have a friendly expert in IT to call for advice whenever we upgrade computers. That is the shining example of how a trustworthy person influences our purchasing intentions.

For every moment of indecision and lack of time or motivation to develop specific competences, we give confidence to a trusted expert's opinion, in order to make our choice more quickly.

In this case, you might need to invest money in hiring him, and you could not have enough available resources. After all, if you are reading this book, you are probably preparing an investor pitch to fund yourself.

You could then get a colleague involved, to join the project's mission, and who could complete the team's missing competencies.

Or you could take advantage of sector research, university reports, or general extended sources that can support your point of view.

According to Aristotle, the second cornerstones of persuasion is the logos: the ability to logically support one's own thesis with facts, data, and statistics.

For example, here is the logos supporting the statement, "Cancer is a relevant problem in the modern society".

Almost 1,000 new cases of cancer are found every day. It is estimated that in Italy, there is approximately 363,000 new diagnosis of cancer during this year (excluding skin cancer, for which it is classified separately, due to the difficulty of clearly distinguishing between causes), about 194,400 (54%) among men and about 168,900 (46%) among women.

This data comes from the Associazione Italiana Registri Tumori (AIRTUM) in 2015.[3]

Taking advantage of numerical data and quantitative sources will help you to establish immovable points supporting your thesis. The numbers speak for themselves, and are not easily rebutted.

The only thing you have to pay attention to when you rely on external sources is quoting quality sources. Avoid basing your entire pitch on statistics taken from Wikipedia!

An alternative is the pilot project. In Lean Startup, Eric Ries talks about Minimum Viable Project (MVP) - a prototype that allows you to validate your hypothesis with minimum investment.

A few years ago, I visited a new local restaurant and was delighted to find an absolutely delicious dish served to me. Intrigued by taste of that dish, I asked the restaurant's owner for the name of the manufacturer in order to obtain the food autonomously. The owner told me the manufacturer supplies only restaurants and hotels with the dish.

The incredible thing was that many online reviews of that restaurant were based around them trying that particular dish.

I imagined an exclusive eCommerce partnership with the manufacturer, and to start a retail channel of distribution. Persuasion would play a fundamental role in the success of the project.

In the agreement with the producer, gaining his consent to proceed become crucial to allow us to start setting out feelers for the business. However, since I don't have any experience in food eCommerce and one of the critical aspects for this type of business is distribution and logistics - another field where I don't have any experience - in order not to risk to lose my only chance, I decided to do two things:

1. Launch an initial test in order to measure the demand and validate the potential of the business

2. Engage a colleague expert in logistics that I know will be interested in the project

To begin, I created a website with catchy graphics of the product and attempted to sell it online. In the beginning, I invested only a few hundred euros into Facebook advertising, in order to attract a small audience and understand the market and saleability of the product.

Why Facebook? Well, Facebook allows me to identify the customers who have eaten in that restaurant, including for sure the ones who have appreciate that product, and to track the demographics and interests of those who click on my advertisements.

Once the user clicks on the advertisement, they're redirected to the website I set up before. Once the universe proceeds to checkout and enters their details, but before payment information is received, the user is redirected to a graphic that says the product has sold out, but promising to let the customer know when the item is available again. This not only creates a database to examine for trends in customers, but creates a potential mailing list for a future release of the product. This information allowed me to create a business plan to present the manufacturer.

---

[3] http://www.airc.it/cancro/cos-e/statistiche-tumori-italia/

To begin distribution of the product, it would take a minimum financial and time investment, but it has the potential to show and measure the demand of the market, and that also demonstrates my ability to sell the product online.

Speaking about the logistics, I already had someone to think about that, so I can move forward with other parts of the plan.

At this stage, it would be enough to prepare a short presentation and propose it to the manufacturer, who would be in front of a team composed of capable people, each able to start a business that is profitable, and with real market evidence based on quantitative tests.

This example allows me to show the concept of minimum viable product, and also allows me to show how possible it is to combine different persuasion techniques in order to build credibility in a real world situation.

Exploiting a prototype to test the market and study potential consumers helps to construct the minimal essential experience for an entrepreneur that is willing to develop an effective solution.

Unfortunately, one of the reasons I see young entrepreneurs losing credibility is the lack of knowledge of the target market. They don't know the people they're trying to sell the product to, or how the product solves the problem for them. For the team to gain experience with potential target markets as soon as possible, is crucial in building credibility, especially if you don't have direct or indirect experiences that allow you to know the audience's habits.

The final consumer's thought is the base upon which to focus your business idea.

Sam Walton, founder of Walmart, said:

"There is only one boss—the customer. And he can fire everybody in the company, from the chairman on down, simply by spending his money somewhere else".[4]

The knowledge of the consumer you speak to is crucial to gaining credibility in front of investors.

During a pitch competition, I once saw a start-up presenting an app for blind people. In short, this app used a phone's camera to recognize kitchen equipment and made the disabled person completely autonomous.

The presentation was entirely made by a person that was wearing sunglasses. At the beginning, I thought that the team wanted to step into the consumer's shoes, but when it was time to show the solution, the conductor took off his sunglasses, took his smartphone from his pocket and showed the usage of the app.

The amazing thing? This person was actually blind and he wasn't a team member. He was a beta tester, a consumer, a user of the app.

Investors were left in awe. The consumer clearly showed the utility of the app in real life to the investors. By having the user speak on behalf of the society, the team proved the importance of the problem and the power of the solution.

[4] Sam Walton, entrepreneur.com

3.2.2 Focus on the audience

To persuade people to change is easier if people understand the benefits of the change. In general, if you want to convince someone to do something, you have to explain them why it's convenient for him to do what you what. In the example of the eCommerce project above, it would be useful to highlight the incremental profitability that the project would gain for him.

It's fine that I trust you and what you do, but if I do something, I am doing it because I want to have a direct benefit from it. Why is it in my best interest for me to proceed?

Remember that people act always in a selfish way and only ever for their own self-interest (S. Sinek).

If you have identified the benefits for the audience, but you don't communicate clearly to them, it will be difficult to obtain the desired results of persuasion.

There is a difference between marketing characteristics and marketing benefits. For example, when Steve Jobs launched the new iPod, he launched a claim that remains written in history: "1000 songs in your pocket".

Jobs didn't speak about the data storage technology, the hard-drive dimensions, or other technicality that made it possible to store such a relatively large number of songs on the device. Jobs knew that the best way to motivate a final customer into buying the iPod was that of making him understand the benefit the iPod gave him: storage. How it was done was a secondary aspect.

Jobs' message was communicated in a clear and simple way. People need to think through swathes of information quickly and, in this case, the claim gives you a shining example of the strength of iPod when compared to its competitors.

In an investor pitch, you have to project your communication, making the investor's benefits clear. In this chapter, you have seen in detail what investors are looking for. When planning the investor pitch, always think about the benefits for the investors, and communicate these points to them in the clearest, simplest, and most direct way. Keep always in mind the audience as the protagonist of the presentation. Remember, there must always be a benefit for them.

But say you don't know the investors, you don't know what they want or what are they looking for in a specific occasion. Before doing your presentation, I suggest you to speak to them directly, if possible, or, to gather as much information about them as possible. The same investors can have different preferences, due to being in different periods of their lives, or taking part on various events.

I once attended a pitch competition, many years ago. The purpose of the jury on that day was to select the most convincing pitch, without any intent of investment, as the prize was a marketing and communications course. In this case, the audience is not trying to maximize the project's return by reducing the risk of investment as much as possible, because, in the end, it is not going to invest. Simply, the best pitch won.

Learn to contextualize, know your audience, and choose the communicated benefits wisely.

3.2.3 Emotionality

Most people are convinced that they make rational decisions, from the daily choice of whether to get up and go to work or sleep in, to the most important ones in our life, such as marriage.
In truth, the basic ingredient at the heart of most of our decisions is emotion. When we find ourselves having to make a decision, we follow a string of emotions tied to recollections, in order to liken the decision we're making as make the choice easier, based on past decisions.[5]

"Most of the brain is constantly busy handling automatic processes. These are all unconscious processes, responsible for an important activity, both emotional and cognitive".[6]

Basically, our brain works on auto pilot most of the time, making us believe we're always attentive, and able to rationally process information and the world around us. In reality, it's the opposite – we're disengaged until something catches our attention, and emotive in all aspects of life.
90% of buying decisions are always related to emotional, unconscious decisions, and not to rational evaluations, as one might think.
Humans have three areas in the brain that interact with one another in every decision you make. Two of them are conscious 'brains', while the other is a subconscious process. Consider the three areas to be three different brains[7]:
1. Lizard brain
2. Mammallian brain
3. Cortical brain
The three brains act autonomously and is out of your control most of the time. I want to show you the functioning of the first two, which are responsible for our emotions.

The lizard brain is the first to be developed in the human being, and is responsible of our survival. It is taking care to avoid danger, whet the appetite, and drive you to reproduce. The lizard brain sends primordial stimulations deeply grafted in the human being and, because of it, they are impossible to be ignored.

Look at this photo:

Figure 1 - Risk of falling

Do you feel like falling? Do you feel unbalanced? Would you unconsciously know where are the beams attached to their foundation, and how far you would have to run to reach safety? It's completely normal to feel a touch of vertigo when looking at the above picture; your lizard brain is protecting you by making you feel fear and encouraging you to crawl to safety as soon as possible. The sensation of vertigo comes immediately and you don't have time to handle and control it; you feel it, and that's it! But, at the same time, they are strong enough to push you to act and, I can assure you, in most cases they succeed.

---

[5] Damasio A., Descartes' Error, Random U.K., 20014
[6] George Loewenstein, professore di psicologia nel dipartimento di scienze sociali alla Carnegie Mellon University, in: Camerer C., Loewenstein G., Prelec D., Neuroeconomics: how neuroscience can inform economics, Journal of Economic Literature, Vol. XLIII, march 2005, cmu.edu

[7] Saletti A., Neuromarketing e scienze cognitive per vendere di più sul web, Dario Flaccovio, 2016

Do you like with the famous lucid effect used? Look how Apple presents the iPhone 7 on its website:

Figure 2 - The lucid effect recalls the water

This effect recalls the water, the essential element to the life. Because of this, your lizard brain turns on and considers the picture as attractive. You feel like you want to take it and use it as soon as possible!

As you can see, the lizard brain's impulses are deep and disruptive, and you can't control them.

What about the mammallian brain, and how can its comprehension of the world help you in your presentations? The mammallian brain governs our emotions. In particular, the thalamus is responsible for managing happiness, sadness and disgust.

I love seeing Pixar animation movies. The movie Inside Out comes to mind especially when talking about conscious and subconscious thought.

Figure 3 - Inside Out, Pixar

The characters represent the emotions in the brain of the protagonist, and each of them is really busy in contributing to Riley's emotional states. I find it simple, funny and brilliant, and a wonderful example of the way the mamillian brain functions.

The part of the mammal brain that we are most concerned about is called amygdala, and it is responsible for associating a memory to every event in your life, both pleasure and pain. If I asked what you ate, and where you were on the 10th of April last year, you probably couldn't answer. But if I asked you where you were last year at on your birthday, if you did something pleasant, the memories would be clear.

This system demonstrates that, if we are excited, we are capable of remembering for a longer period of time.

Because of this, it's essential to know how to act on the audience's emotions, especially during the attack phase of the presentation, when the peak of attention is free falling.

Activating the amygdala is crucial to moving your audience towards the point of desire to assist. The desire is regulated by the production of dopamine and serotonin.

Dopamine is commonly referred to as the 'rewarding molecule'; it is produced when you feel happy about something you have done. Think about receiving positive feedback for your service, an investor that is interested on your work, etc.

Social networks are alive thanks to the constant production of dopamine. When you post a photo and you wait for likes, you're producing dopamine the more little clicks people give you. Any chance is a good chance to check if your friends like it, if someone has commented it, how many people had interacted with it, and so on, causing a lowly-rising tide of dopamine in the brain.[8]

Serotonin is commonly referred to as the 'molecule of love', and makes us experience attraction. It is proven that seeing pictures of people we relate to produces serotonin. This mechanism is connected with the feeling of belonging to a group that has always been the basis of human survival.

This is the reason why we use images of people to boost the storytelling parts contained in a presentation.

Recently, I ended up in the website, *https://www.lensabl.com*, start-up that sells spectacle lenses. The thing that caught my eye was the use of close-ups of normal people, in video, that shows you their glasses.

Figure 4 - https://www.lensabl.com

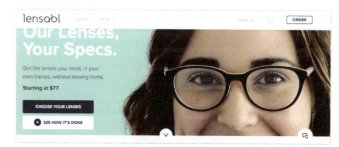

Figure 5 - https://www.lensabl.com

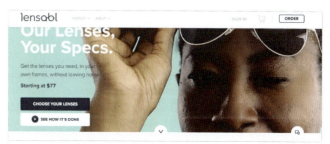

Figure 6 - https://www.lensabl.com

If you wait on the site for a few seconds, you will see that there are different people alternating.

[8] Ricerca di Mauricio Delgado, associate professor of psychology at Rutgers University in Newark, N.J. Per approfondimenti: Soat Molly, Social media triggers a dopamine high, ama.org

This is a shining example of how we try to move the consumer by making him feel like part of the group. By showing different people, Lensabl is trying to represent as wide a range of targets as possible, in order to strike the most potential end users.

It is crucial to emotionally engage the audience, to encourage the decisional process of investing in your start-up.

How can you create contents that move the audience in a so deep way to get it involved on an emotion level?

One of the techniques consists of creating contents that could make the people listening revisit past experiences. People decide according to past experiences, driven by sensations that they already have in their memory.

> **J. Conger says:**
>
> *"Without emotion, every attempt at persuasion is meant to fail. But by showing too much, can be as much counterproductive as being too little involved. The most important strategy to remember is to get connected, showing the same emotions as the audience".* [9]

People feel close to someone who shows something similar to them, and they instinctively develop an attitude of trust.

Human beings have the innate ability of trusting our peers, not just people with whom you have shared something, but also with whom you have only a physical resemblance, or the same name.

Randy Garner, in a study conducted at the Sam Houston State University[10], has demonstrated that the name of a person can influence the attitude of people around them.

During the experiment, Randy asked a class of 82 students to read a short story and answer a questionnaire, the purpose of which was to understand how much the reader appreciated the protagonist. Half of the students had a story where the protagonist's name was Kerry, while in the other half, the protagonist's name was the same as the reader. Therefore, excluding the students that had Kerry as main character, the others had a protagonist with a name similar to their own.

The result of the experiment was that the students that evaluated the protagonist with a similar name to them gave, on average, higher scores than the others. This research demonstrated that, when we feel similar to someone else, we tend to appreciate him more, even if this is due to a casual or insignificant reason.

In general, we tend to consider trustworthy the people with whom we have one or more common traits.[11]

Imagine you're abroad for a holiday. Suddenly, you realize to have lost your ID, maybe it was stolen in the metro, or it fell out of your pocket.

Without ID, you could have problems taking the flight back home, and you find yourself in a difficult situation. You immediately go to a police station to file a report, but neither you nor the local officer speak a common tongue.

When you arrive at the police station, an officer from your own country who moved abroad on business welcomes you.

---

[9] Conger I., The necessary art of persuasion, hbr.org

[10] Garner R., Name Similarity and persuasion, Sam Houston State University

Instinctively, you feel safer and you feel like you can count on that person.

This story helps you recall that reassuring sensation of finding someone 'of your group'—generally speaking, people tend to trust other people, assuming that they share something with them.

For this reason, you must play strategically when you have to create a context shared with your investors. The aim is to demonstrate you have something in common in order to push investors into considering your team trustworthy. From here comes the importance of knowing your audience. If you want to draw a common context and show you're the same as your investors, you must absolutely know what context results in common ground with the people in your audience.

It's extremely effective to tell a story, a metaphor or an anecdote in which the audience can see itself, in order to trigger an emotional connection. If you can make the audience experience the same emotions as the protagonist, then it means that you have hooked them and that they are ready to listen to you completely.

> "When a child falls down, the parents suffer at the same time. Our favorite soccer player messes up the perfect goal, we get upset. Watching a dancer feels exhilarating to us. The so-called mirror neurons, a widespread nervous system in our brain, are responsible for these feelings. The proximity of other people activates these nerve cells and recreates the mirror image of the condition or emotions of the other person within us. This means, if we are watching someone, our brain reacts as if we were active".
>
> "Mirror neurons are also responsible for our desire to imitate the behavior of others. Apple's iPod and its white ear buds are the perfect example for the influence of mirror neurons on our purchasing behavior. Before the iPod era, headphones and wires were available only in black".
>
> "When we see a person wearing unusual headphones our mirror neurons spark the desire within us to get the same trendy earphones".
>
> **Martin Lindstrom**[12]

When you use a story or an anecdote, you must make the audience view itself as the protagonist, in order to make them experience his same emotions. The main character could be you, a consumer that is experiencing the problem and can, then, feel its emotions. The main thing is that you and the audience feel connected.

The audience has to see itself as the protagonist and has to feel that you share that experience too, or because it's you, or because you are connected with the character. That way, the audience will trust you.

---

[11] Byrne D., Ervin C.R., Lamberth J., Continuity between the experimental study of attraction and real-life computer dating, Journal of Personality and Social Psychology, 16(1), 1970, psycnet.apa.org

[12] Martin Lindstrom, 90 percent of all purchasing decisions are made subconsciously, mag.ispo.com

Imagine the story as a bridge that connects you and your audience. On one hand, is crucial that you are connected to the story to show that you are at the same level as the people in your audience. On the other hand, the audience must view itself in the story in order to experience the same emotions.

Figure 7 - The story is a bridge that emotionally connects you with the audience

The third part of Aristotle's plan persuade talks about pathos, referring to the reactions experienced by the listener. According to Aristotle, persuasion is produced by the mood of the audience when the speech makes them feel some kind of passions. In fact, he claims that people judge in a different way, depending on whether they feel pain, pleasure, friendship, or hate.

Emotions influence the human judge and it's for this reason that, if they are used intelligently, they can help to persuade the audience and to engrave a message in their memories. For Aristotle, the beginning and the end of the speech are, definitely, the most important parts. To trigger these emotions, according to Aristotle, we can use a metaphor or a short story, or we can take advantage of some kind of emotionally-strong interlayer.

Let's take as example the famous Alfred's pitch, start-up winner of the Disrupt 2014, with a total earning of $12.5million.

"Good morning, my name is Marcela Sapone, I am the co-founder of Alfred and I am here to give you back the most precious resource you have: time".

You can already notice the opening and the effect by which Marcela locks onto the audience's attention. Everybody would like to get back their time and, therefore, everyone is interested in knowing how to do that.

"First, let me tell you about Dan. He is busy, he works hard and gets home late to a messy and dirty apartment".

Figure 8 - Dan's home in a turmoil

At this point, Marcela introduces the story of Dan, a guy that doesn't have time to take care of his apartment.

"Dan stumbles over his laundry…"

"He wakes up the next morning and sees a stack of dishes. When he goes looking for the cereal, he realizes he's finished them".

Figure 9 - The dirty plates in the morning

"Dan needs help. Dan needs Alfred!"

Figure 10 - Introduction of the solution

"Finally, the luxury of personal service for the rest of us. For $99 per month, Dan can get his very own Alfred that, once a week, every week, on set days, will take care of his housekeeping needs".

Marcela introduces the solution and motivates with the reason why Alfred is better than the solutions currently available on the market. Then she launches a live demo, during which she shows the use of the application.

In the end, she comes back to the story and makes the final step, the most important one...

"Dan can finally get back home, eat his cereal and he doesn't have to think about housekeeping problems anymore. But Dan isn't the only one. Working parents, professionals, each of us, can be like Dan and have our own personal Alfred".

Marcela has connected the audience to the protagonist, explaining why the story of Dan is the story of each of us, and why we need this solution.
This is a fundamental moment of the initial storytelling, because it's the moment where the speaker makes feel the audience like part of the story. Probably a good share of the audience was already seen itself as part of the story but now, without any doubt, every single person is part of it.

"Let's see now what the people that trusted us are saying".

Figure 11 - Alfred testimonials

By showing the reviews left by the actual customers, Marcela closes the circle and earns credibility by taking advantage of the element of the social evidence. After all, if there are people so happy to testify it, the service must be top-notch! Moreover, seeing that the customers leave comments makes everyone understand that the project is functional and that it satisfies the market perfectly.
Marcela has combined emotional elements with elements that are part of her credibility and, at the same time, she managed to take advantage of a common feature many of the investors share: the lack of time to dedicate to housekeeping. Do you see how the conjunction of the three key principles of persuasion contributes to an enhancement of your communication strategy?

3.3 STORYTELLING FOR PRESENTATIONS

When I started to deal with presentation design, I remember one of the most misleading things was this *"through story"* approach to the communicative structure of a presentation. On one hand, everyone was saying that you have to start with a story in order to connect with the audience, but, on the other hand, it is hard to understand how to build a story that truly works.

Stories are a natural tool, common to everyone, as the basis of human communication, but that doesn't mean that we are all able to tell engaging stories.

I don't want to make you a *master storyteller,* but it is important that you are able to rapidly structure a short story, a metaphor or an anecdote, relevant to and regarding your idea of start-up and that could touch the investors.

Moreover, since time is a scarce resource, I would like you to succeed in the most efficient way.

For this reason, I want to share with you a very powerful and easy-to-apply model that can be used to create immersive stories.

I'm referring to Dr. Andrew V. Abela's model, which is discussed in his book, The Presentation.

For example: *Shrek is a green ogre who lives alone in a wooden house in a swamp, taking showers with mud and scaring everyone who gets too close to him.*

In the meantime, all the creatures of the fairy tales, including Pinocchio, the Big Bad Wolf of Little Red Riding Hood, Snow White, the Seven Dwarves and the Three Little Pigs, are being exiled from Duloc, Lord Farquaad's fief. Lord Farquaad is a pretty short man, but equally clever and cruel, who wants to rise to power as a king.

All the condemned characters are forced into Shrek's swamp. This is intolerable for Shrek, and so the ogre decides to leave in search of Lord Farquaad.
[…]

All the stories begin with the description of the context (Situation)—the famous "Once Upon a Time" - and the introduction of the characters. In this case, the story begins with the presentation of the protagonist.

The next step is always the problem. Something happens in the plot of the story, that influences the protagonist and forces him to undertake a change. On this occasion, the fairytale characters exiled from the fief and lodged in his swamp create a difficult situation to which he must necessarily respond.

At this point, the solution is introduced. Shrek, in order to solve the problem, heads towards Lord Farquaad's fief. The story then continues, and is intertwined with other characters and problems that Shrek will have to solve in order to come back to his swamp as a winner.

The story will be a repeat of the model Problem-Solution.

Andrew Abela calls this model "chiama il suo modello", or S.Co.R.E. (Situation, Complication, Resolution, Example).

Did you notice that there is a fourth step?

As Abela says in his book, the business world is made by numbers and abstract concepts for which, when we tell a story, it is always useful to add an example. The example allows you to give a break to the audience between a resolution and the next problem. Otherwise, there is the risk that the story becomes too overwhelming.

In business, the example also assumes the role of making the solution credible by supporting the thesis, maybe with authoritative quotes or numerical data and reliable sources. In the case of an investor pitch, the model S.Co.R.E. is a crucial tool to structure an effective presentation.

In the beginning, we define the context where you operate and this can be done through an elevator pitch, or through one or more dedicated slides which introduce the investors to your world. Following that is a problem, or a set of more problems that you set yourself to solve with your start-up idea.

If the story is built correctly and you were able to communicate it, giving the audience the right emotions, you will produce the necessary attention to introduce your solution.

Obviously, the solution must the believable to the eyes of investors (see product-solution fit, Steve Blank)[13] and because of that, you will need to provide information in support. For example, mockups show the product or tests with clients or results of traction.

---

[13] Blank S., The Four Steps to the Epiphany, K&S Ranch, 2013

Among the pitches that I have analyzed, there is one that struck me in the way it structured the initial storytelling: the pitch of pinmypet ($771k collected in 3 round).

The initial slide includes the elevator pitch:

Figure 12 - Cover slide with elevator pitch

Thanks to this slide, it is already clear that this presentation is about a tracking device for pets. With the first slide, even without speaking, the founders soaked the investors in their world.

This is an example of intelligent application of the elevator pitch in the cover slide, projected even before the front man started speaking.

The first slide after the cover is a contextual one. Julia and her beloved dog! We can see that they are happy together.

Figure 13 - The Situation

Then we immediately get into the problem: the dog is lost and Julia is desperate.

Figure 14 - The Problem

Moreover, thanks to the two slides that show the sign about the lost dog, the founders make it immediately clear what solution their pitch will be proposing.

The sight of the sign makes you think that it is an old and clearly ineffective solution. The girl that cries for the loss of her dog carries a strong emotion to the audience.

We have explained the problem, gambling on the emotional investment of people. Now statistics that reinforce the importance of the problem are introduced.

Figure 15 - Data that support the problem

The loss of the dog could have happened to anyone amongst the investors who have or once had a pet. However, the size of the problem tells the investors why they should care about this theme. In this way, the founders are sure to gain the attention of the audience, both as people and investors. After maximizing the audience's attention and having raised their expectations, the team is ready to present the solution. With the first slide, they show the solution; with the second one, they give a first example.

Figure 16 - The Solution

The model S.Co.R.E. helps you to create an effective story to start your presentation with. The model is extremely easy to apply and is a very comfortable tool to use every time we have to prepare the beginning of an effective pitch.

The rest of the presentation will follow the model S.Co.R.E. The context is defined once, but from the solution can arise a series of doubts in the audience that could question the solution, the market, the business model, the team, and so on.

Usually, the doubts match the questions that the audience is having in that moment. Since it is not possible to answer all the questions immediately, we must predict what the questions will be and then create slides to answer in an orderly manner.

Which doubt could come into question to the investors at this stage of the presentation of Pinmypet?

Probably they will be wondering what is the business model, or if the team has all the necessary internal resources. For this reason, there will be for sure slides supporting the mentioned points. The more doubts you manage to anticipate and clarify, the more the presentation will be effective.

3.4 FOUR TECHNIQUES TO DEFINITELY "NOT PERSUADE"

If so far, I have talked about all the techniques useful to turn a simple conversation into a persuasive message that could affect the behavior of the audience. Now I want to show you some behaviors that might surely undermine your efforts.

To put the persuasion techniques into practice is not easy, because it requires experience and intuition. While you are refining these abilities, let's see what you absolutely should not do when you present your pitch.

3.4.1 Being impatient

Figure 17 - Being impatient

Persuasion requires time and, even in a presentation of a few minutes, it is necessary to lead your audience through a path that motivates them to change.

You may have closed millionaire rounds, you may have a lot of experience and excellent traction, but that doesn't allow you to open a presentation with an explicit request of what you want.

Do not make the mistake to hurry to what you want. If you reveal immediately the call to action, whether it is a funding request, a strategic partnership or something else, you will give the audience a target to attack from the beginning, if they don't agree with your ideas.

The necessity of persuasion comes from the fact that people will not change by themselves. So, it is pretty easy to be facing a skeptical audience, especially in the beginning.

Learn to be patient, follow the communication plan you have developed meticulously. Conduct the audience through the presentation, go beyond the barriers of change, don't uncover your position and keep going to the end. When the audience will be ready, launch your call to action.

3.4.2 Do not accept compromise

Figure 18 - Who doesn't listen and doesn't make compromises

Reardon Kathlee[14], Professor at the Southern California University, says that rarely can a person influence another without being willing to change their point of view during the negotiation.

A predominant part of the persuasion process is listening. If your audience feels that you are taking their point of view into consideration, and that you are trying to find a solution that benefits both of you, he will surely be more likely to adopt your point of view.

Otherwise, if the audience understands that you are only trying to make him change without being open to a change yourself, you will lose his trust and you will significantly increase the probability of failure.

Remember that the dimension of the funding that you ask for will have to be paid in something. Traditionally, the Venture Capital Funds invest in equity, and that is the company's shares.

But how many shares is asking a VC for a determined amount invested? To answer this question, we will have to enter in the world of due diligence. However, at this point I am only interested in specifying that the answer depends on the result of the negotiation process between the start-up and the Investment Fund.

In fact, you, entrepreneur, will have to conduct a negotiation that enhances your company's shares as much as possible. When you have to undergo these negotiation processes, remember that the VC will join with a point of view opposite yours. He will want to buy a share for as cheap as he can get away with. It's your job to negotiate a bigger price.

However, asserting yourself too forcefully and not being open to negotiation will put you at risk to fail the negotiation, and maybe lose interested investment opportunities.

In other words, during the negotiation process, you will not only have to be open to hearing the other parties out, but also to be willing to merge others' points of view with your final aim.

3.4.3 Acting in a short-term approach

Figure 19 – The Ant and the Grasshopper

---

[14] http://www.kathleenkelleyreardon.com

Pitching is a process that follows the entrepreneur through the hole life-cycle of his company. The metrics will change, the front man's experience will change (by failing, failing and failing again!), the audience will change, the circumstances, the purpose of the pitch, the dimension of the funding, and so on.

Moreover, by being a start-up, and so being in a dynamic and fast-developing environment, it is reasonable to expect that the presentation of the business will change just as rapidly.

A common mistake is thinking that the pitch is a "once in a lifetime" presentation. Do not wait for the day in which you don't have enough money to keep going in order to start pitching. Above all, do not stop pitching as soon as you have obtained your first funding.

The funding path will always go along with the start-up, from the day of its birth.

Learn to think about pitching as a long-term path and plan your communications by looking to the future. Furthermore, remember that the investor pitch is a presentation that is an initial incentive to start a mutual understanding path with the investors. Nobody will finance you at the end of your presentation; findings and more-in-depth analysis will follow.

Do not condense an entire business plan into those few slides presented to the investor. You don't need it. Focus instead on the essential information that is useful to make your audience curious and convince them to investigate further.

3.4.4 Believe that the presentation is everything

Figure 20 - Slides are important but it's the people that make a difference

Surely the slides of an investor pitch are crucial to the success of a presentation. There are no doubts so far. Without a well-structured, simple, direct and complete deck, it will be really difficult to move the audience.

However, good slides aren't enough for the success of the presentation on their own. They play a crucial role, but are still on the back burner. In fact, slides allow the relater to shine in front of the audience, they increase his value, and help him make his messages indelible in people's memory. Slides are important, but it's the people that make a difference. You are the key to the success of the persuasion process.

Therefore, prepare yourself adequately and, if you are afraid to talk to the audience, or if you don't think you're able to give a convincing presentation, think about who in your team can do it in your place.

Learn to consider the presentation as a combination of elements: slides and public speaking.

3.5 Summarizing

We can summarize the art of persuasion in three key points, in agreement with Jay A. Conger:

- **CREDIBILITY**

To be convincing you must first be credible. To build your credibility you need to know the topic or to have personal / professional relationships that demonstrate you are aware of the topic

- **FOCUS ON THE AUDIENCE**

Highlight the benefits to the audience and motivate why they should adopt your ideas. Remember that people are reluctant to change, so you'll have to walk the extra mile to persuade them

- **EMOTIONS**

As we said, most of the time people make impulsive decisions driven by the emotions. Learn how to deeply touch the audience so that your messages will profoundly affect them

4
CHAPTER

THE PITCH: AN EFFICIENT STRUCTURE

An efficient pitch must represent and heighten the reality that it describes. Thus, a good pitch must be "woven" into the firm that is being presented and into its specificities: strong points and weak points. I don't think there's a pitch that works for everyone, because every reality needs a specific presentation.

Moreover, a pitch about a startup constantly evolves as a function of the following: of the rapidly changing results; of the audience to which it is targeted; of the objectives to be reached; and from the dynamic reality of an innovative firm that grows at a very fast pace.

But then how can we find order in this *maremágnum* of presentations, if, even inside of the same company, there are multiple pitches?

The investor pitch must be essential. How then can one be sure of including the truly fundamental information that would convince the investor?

Even the sequence with which the information is presented effects the result. What then should one say first, and what afterwards?

In this chapter, we will cover together the route versus the definition of a structure, which will serve as a starting point for organizing your content and best presenting your startup.

4.1 INVESTOR PITCH OR BUSINESS PLAN?

If, like me, you've found yourself in the situation of having to deliver a pitch, you probably know what I refer to when I have to select what aspects of our activity I should relate to the investors.

In fact, being immersed, with your rhythms as a startupper, in your entrepreneurial adventures, it's often burdensome to expend sweat and sacrifices in order to create very few essential concepts for the investor, and you risk confusing the pitch with the completed business plan.

Figure 1 - Investor pitch vs Business plan

4.1.1 Business plan

The business plan is a document that exhaustively describes all the aspects of your business activities. It is usually presented as a long report and often, depending on the subject matter, can contain an enormous amount of content. As such, the business plan can require a lot of time to be analyzed.

It involves a document that, being by nature an exhaustive report, doesn't need a supervisor and the contents of which are best understood by the reading of it.

The business plan helps you to completely illustrate all the entrepreneurial activity and your vision for your product. As a matter of fact, it often contains a huge mass of (uninteresting) details for an investor that has come into contact with the project for the first time.

Being a document that takes some time to be analyzed, and often anonymous, the business plan is used according to the interest demonstrated by an investor that would finance the activity.

I would strongly discourage you from using it as a document for hooking or enticing the investor; it would require too great a force on the part of the reader, who would probably end up discarding it, rendering all your sacrifices wasted.

4.1.2 Investor pitch

The investor pitch, on the other hand, is a brief presentation that serves to attract the immediate attention of the investor, with the precise scope of pushing him to delve deeper into the material.

This is an extremely important point of attention: henceforth, you must always keep in mind that no investor will finance you right after the presentation of the pitch, as, even in the best case, he would still need to dive further into the details in order to carry out adequate due diligence. To present the pitch, you often have very little time, and usually find yourself presenting in true competition with other startups.

Generally, a presentation of a pitch lasts 5-10 minutes - at most.

You will have to bear in mind that, in such little time, it would be impossible to clarify all the necessary and natural doubts of the investor that would enable him to make the decision to finance your activity.

By these considerations, you can already guess that the pitch shouldn't contain all the details of the activity, but only those essential for reaching the objective of generating this initial curiosity.

Lastly, the pitch has the arduous job of standing you out amongst all the other combative entrepreneurs that present their pitches before and after you.

If you have experienced a pitch competition, you already have in mind what I'm talking about. In the competitions, one may find oneself inconveniently fixed into a tiny slot of 5 minutes (if not less) in the middle of a line of other projects.

Try to descend from the stage and put yourself in the shoes of those poor people that see 15 or 20 projects in the space of a day.

I can guarantee you that after the first 2 or 3 presentations, they start to all seem identical and the threshold of attention falls. The only way to win them back over is by surprising them.

As the audience grows more and more tired, it becomes more difficult to wake them. You will need a truly sensational effect or surprise.

The natural conclusion is that, if in those few minutes at your disposition, you're not able to immediately capture the attention of your audience, you risk reaching the end of your presentation without being listened to, and certainly won't have created the best conditions for undertaking a process of gathering funds.

4.2 WHAT IS AN ELEVATOR PITCH?

At the start of my entrepreneurial journey, during an accelerated program in London, I remember an exceptional presentation by one of my mentors.

At the end of the presentation, all the startuppers wanted to have a meeting with her, and thus we found ourselves in a queue to ask her for an appointment.

Unfortunately, the mentor was on her way and hadn't planned to dedicate time to activities with the startups, so she said she would meet more teams quickly before lunch. I happened to be there at the exact time in which she decided to go to lunch, and so she told me that she wouldn't have more time for my project. However, she told me that, if in the elevator from the 4th floor to the basement I were able to interest her, I would be able to have lunch with her. Otherwise, she would go down the elevator and I would return to the 4th floor with all the others.

I was able to convince her, and she asked me to accompany her when the doors of the elevator closed. What she told me during lunch was interesting, but what she had to teach me had already been taught to me in the elevator before arriving at lunch. The way in which I was able to strike her was that which in literature is defined as *an elevator pitch:*

"A view of an idea, a product, a service, a project, a person or another solution, and is projected to initiate initial conversation".[1]

According to Investopedia, the elevator pitch is defined as: *"A slang term used to describe a brief speech that outlines an idea for a product, service or project. The name comes from the notion that the speech should be delivered in the short time period of an elevator ride, usually 20-60 seconds".*[2]

In essence, the elevator pitch is a potent communicative instrument for interesting someone in a very brief space of time, generating curiosity and desire to know more.
For this reason, the elevator pitch is brief, as very little time is available and, as defined by Chris O'Leary, it is useful for sparking up a conversation.

In the preceding chapter, I spoke to you about how important it is to be ready and available to make one's pitch, by gaining experience through continuous practice.
Now I can add that you never know when the opportunity comes; it might be that it arrives when you least expect it. Indeed, it usually happens this way!

Maybe you're in a lift with the partner of a big investment fund just as you're coming home one evening. In those moments, you have to be ready to speak in a very short time, or risk losing the opportunity of a lifetime.
Therefore, I would advise that you straighten the antennae and read the next few lines attentively.

An effective elevator pitch is composed of 3 parts[3]:

BENEFIT

The benefit is the reason for which your listener should be interested in your project. Remember that people are interested in that which helps them, that which resolves their problems and simplifies their lives.
When speaking with a client or a business, the ideal act is that which connects the benefit to an economic and financial metric.

Suppose you're developing an intelligent central unit that would allow for the optimization of electrical consumption in hotels.

---

[1] O'Leary C., Elevator Pitch Essentials: How to Get Your Point Across in Two Minutes or Less, The Limb Press, 2008

[2] Elevator pitch, investopedia.com
[3] Geoffrey James, How to give a flawless elevator pitch, inc.com

Wrong approach:
- We work in the world of tourism to improve electrical consumption (too generic)
- We build an energy saving central unit (too generic and missing the benefit)

Correct approach:
- Hotels use our central line to reduce their electrical consumption by 50% every year
- Hotels depend on us for reducing their energy costs by a million euros every year

So the benefit must be specific and significant for the listener.

DIFFERENTIATING FACTOR

The reason why you are the best solution to the problem of the listener. It answers the question "Why you, and not another person?".

Wrong approach:
- We are the market leader (so you say!)
- We are quicker than competitor "x" (again, so you say!)
- We would be happy to be able to tell you about our project (doesn't concern me)

Right approach
- We have a patent that protects the algorithm of energy optimization (patents, as a system of protection of one's intellectual property, often act as a very potent differentiating factor that immediately attracts the attention of the investor)

CALL TO ACTION

The CTA is the true scope of the elevator pitch, and that is the request for a useful meeting to bring the details into consideration. In those 20-60 seconds at your disposal, the most precious thing you can obtain from your listener is more of his time in future to go further.
Consider that it's truly improbable that an investor would decide to finance you after being struck by 30 seconds of elevator pitch right after the doors of an elevator open. As such concentrate on the objectives and ask the right thing. So focus on the goal and ask the right questions.

Wrong approach
- This is my business card, call me if you're interested (you're not asking anything)
- If you leave me your email address I'll send you a business plan (calm down, buddy, you're going too fast)
- As we're still in the process of financing, would you like to finance us? (now you're just being silly)

Right approach:
- How do you feel about meeting up next week to discuss more in detail?
- You seem interested, would you be free during the week to learn more?

Shall we try and put it all together?
You get into the elevator and recognize the investor.

You: *Are you (full name) of (company)?*

Investor: *Yes, I am she, and who might you be?*

You: *I patented a central unit that hotels use to reduce energy wastage by 50 percent every year.*

Investor: *Interesting. And how does it work, exactly?*

You: *I would like to describe the solution to you in detail, would you be available this week?*

What do you think? Could it work?

Consider that this is an example that I invented, with the purpose of showing you how the efficiency of an elevator pitch depends on your ability to make it simple and conversational.

The approach that I have shown you is very simple, and the formula will allow you to create a complete and efficient elevator pitch. Nevertheless, the presentation alone won't be able to exactly transpose all the necessary text.

Thus, one of the more recurring forms of the elevator pitch is a small phrase in the introduction slide that is projected while the supervisor takes his position on the stage. The slide normally serves the function of describing the context and managing the expectations of the public.

Welcome   1

AirBed&Breakfast

Book rooms with locals, rather than hotels.

Figure 2 - Elevator pitch in from slide cover for Airbnb

Now that you have seen how an elevator pitch is prepared, take time to develop your own. Go to the mirror and try it 'til it is perfect. At this point, place it in a safe corner of your memory and keep it ready for the next occasion.

4.3 WHAT INFORMATION TO INCLUDE IN A PITCH

You should have already begun to guess that there are three major aspects of the pitch to take into consideration:

1. Which contents to include, and in what order to present them

2. How to communicate the contents so as to capture and maintain the attention of the investor for those few moments of your presentation

3. How to visualize the contents on the slide

In this section, we will clarify the first point, treating the other points in dedicated sections further ahead.
The first time that I found myself having to deal with the problem of what to put in the presentation, my reaction was very simple: a Google search on how to structure an effective investor pitch.

At the time, I thought that it would have been simple to find an index supported by some famous investment fund or some important business accelerator/incubator to rapidly resolve the problem.

It would have been very simple this way. It would have been enough to take a replicable index on my PowerPoint and then place the context within.

However, the first thing I saw, after clicking 'go', was a great quantity of random information, presented one after another.

Figure 3 - Searching on the Internet for a structure of a pitch to use generates too much discordant information

As you can imagine, being an oft-discussed theme, everyone proposes his or her own version and thus you find yourself facing proposals by investment funds of varying fame, by business accelerators or incubators, by bloggers that gather famous startup pitches, or by influencers that speak of theirs.

In this sea of information, you will realize the difficulty of having to make a choice by necessity. After all, it isn't easy to confront and decide on the material only on the basis of the fame of the fund or the researched accelerators.

Thus, I decided to gather the largest number of investor pitches possible that can be found, only with the purpose of analyzing them and, above all, of dealing with them.

I concentrated on the most successful pitches, those that have enabled prosperous entrepreneurial realities and opened significant routes to financing.

Below is a representation of the collection of the structures of pitches:

Figure 4 - Structures of successful investor pitch compared

As was already seen in the phase of the Google search, the structure is different among these pitches, but, with a more attentive look, one begins to notice interesting similarities.

In attempting to give a color code to the similar sections, a more defined map of the contents begins to emerge.

Figure 5 - Common points between the structures of the successful investor pitches.

Quantifying successively the presence and the order of the appearance of each section, a first logical sequence of the contents can be defined.
In fact, through a qualitative analysis, it is possible to identify a pattern on the basis of the number of times in which a determined section appears in a specific position within the diverse presentations.

This allows us to define a trace that we can reasonably follow to structure an investor pitch.

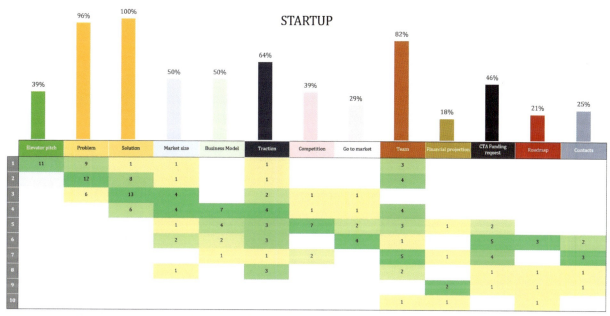

Figure 6 - Result of the analysis of the successful startup pitches

The histogram represented above the table indicates the percentage of the section present on the survey of the analyzed pitches. For example, problem and solution are presented in almost all the pitches of the survey, between 96% and 100%, the teams also appears for 82% of presentations.

The force of the Problem/Solution combination thus sticks out immediately and the dominant presence of the team. These three are the load-bearing columns of the pitch. If you think about it for a moment, you will realize that it's quite reasonable as a result. Simply by thinking that, with this structure you would be able to explain the problem that you want to resolve, the solution that you intend to adopt and who would be involved.

As you will see through the course of the book, these are the basis for potent storytelling.

After all, ideas are important (problem/solution), but people make the difference (team). Above all, in the initial phases, when the startup still exists in form of an idea or a prototype and the first responses from the market are, in reality, only tests on the consumers, investors cannot help but evaluate if the team has the force and ability to realize the form.

"If you give a good idea to a mediocre team, they will screw it up. If you give a mediocre idea to a brilliant team, they will either fix it, or throw it away and come up with something better"

Ed Catmull, [4]
Founder of Pixar & President at Walt Disney

[4] Catmull E., Creativity Inc.: Overcoming the unseen forces that stand in the way of true inspiration, Random house, 2014

The traction section reveals this to be present in more than half of the pitches analyzed. In this case, however, it is necessary to specify that this section depends strongly on the stage of maturity of the project.

For a project that is still too young, it will be difficult to define the data of traction, as often the solution has not yet been realized and there isn't neither a prototype that might be able to compare even the initial responses.
Obviously, it has to do with a fundamental section within a pitch, and it allows for the increase of your credibility before the investors.

What is curious is the presence of the elevator pitches in the first 39%. It means that the entrepreneurs preferred to make it immediately clear what it is they do, ahead of even starting the presentation.

In studying the graph, it can therefore be seen that there are different, more important sections within an investor pitch, that present themselves with variable appearance.
This consideration confirms to us that there isn't a pitch that works for all, and that on the basis of these cases, we need to look further into a section, rather than into another, so as to maximize the communicative efficiency of your message to the investor.

The table above, with respect to the graph, indicates the number of occurrences of the section in correspondence to its position within the presentation. This data allows us to give an order to the diverse sections of the pitch.
For example, there is an evident concentration of the elevator pitch section at the start of the presentation; that is quite reasonable, as it is openly seen, to avoid all doubt, that it explains quickly what your project does.
What follows is a revelation of an important presence of the sections characterized by the Problem/Solution combination and so on, up to the financial projection finale.

The market size section is demonstrated as very present between the third and the fourth positions of the presentation, without having a dominant position. That notwithstanding, the section positions itself naturally at the top, giving a measure of the economic potential of the project, supporting the observance of the solution (Is there a market for the proposed solution, and if so, how big is it?)

The request for financing (CTA Funding request), on the other hand, seems very present between the sixth and seventh position, but given that it deals with the final call to action, the object of the pitch, its natural position is still at the end of the presentation.

Even Roadmap and Contact struggle to find themselves visibly, but it's quite intuitive to assign them the final positions and closure of the presentation. The roadmap serves to give a future vision and manage the expectations of the investor, while contact refers to the contacts of the person with which one may communicate, in case of eventual interest in further connection on the part of the investor.

Usually, by contact, it is enough to add one's own contact information to the cover and closure slides.

At the heart of the analysis of these first investors, a structure of a common fund begins to reveal itself.

Nevertheless, the pitch presentations of real cases often reveal themselves to be incomplete and with varying lengths. This negatively effects the comparison of one with the other.

As such, I decided to bring the analysis forward, enriching it with another typology of investor pitch gathered, that is the structure recommended by influential persons, gurus and professionals with experience in the sector.

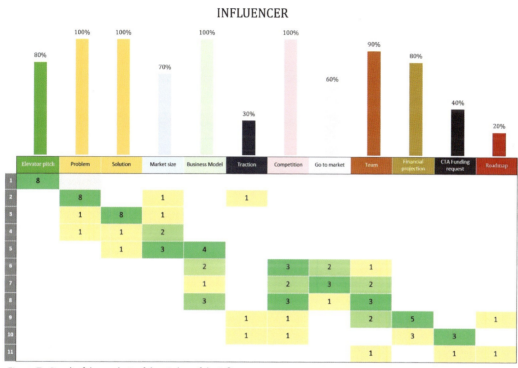

Figure 7 - Result of the analysis of the pitches of the influencers

Sensational! The structure that emerges from this second analysis shows similarities evident with that formulated by the real start up investor pitches. Here is what we're starting to extrapolate: an efficient structure to construct a winning investor pitch. That notwithstanding, a few interesting differences reveal themselves. The distribution of the sections is much less fragmented and appears immediately cleared compared to other sections, and may be present with much higher scores compared to the preceding analysis: Elevator pitch, Problem, Solution, Business Model, Team, Financial Projection.

From the preceding analysis, some doubt could remain toward starting the presentation with an Elevator Pitch. Instead, it's very clear that the influencers (amongst whom we would number important investors) want to know immediately what is being spoken about.

That, obviously, does not leave aside the approach of introducing the pitch, presenting the problem and the solution, but the attack must immediately give the idea of that which is spoken of.

CTA, Funding request and Roadmap place themselves more precisely towards the end of the presentation, in the same position in which we had though to place them in the preceding analysis.

Traction instead remains more uncertain, and thus less present in the analyzed survey. We have already seen that this section can vary in function of the stage of maturity of the business. Finally, the section contact is absent. Discreetly adding contacts in the closing slide doesn't, however, weigh down the pitch. Personally, I am of the opinion that it's useful to an investor that may want to contact you. Therefore, I would suggest to keep it within the conclusive structure.

4.4 THE PERFECT STRUCTURE FOR A SUCCESSFUL INVESTOR PITCH

The compared analysis of the structures of investor pitches coming from real successful cases, with more theoretical structures derived from the plurennial experiences of experts of the sector, has allowed us to condense data originating from numerous sources into a single and definitive structure, to be used to inform your next pitch presentations.

Below is the obtained structure:

1. Elevator pitch
2. Problem
3. Solution
4. Market size
5. Business Model
6. Traction
7. Competition
8. Go to market
9. Team
10. Financial projection
11. CTA Funding request
12. Roadmap
13. Contact

4.5 Summarizing

We have analyzed investor pitches coming from famous successful cases and have extrapolated a common structure out of them.

Thereafter, we have analyzed the pitch structures suggested by famous influencers and investors of the startup world.

Comparing the structures derived from the first and the second case, we have identified similarities that have enabled us to define a recommended structure.

The structure of the investor pitch drawn up assures you completeness of information and communicative efficiency.
In fact, following the list of the sections meticulously, you avoid the risk of forgetting something. Respecting the order of the sections, you will be certain of using the best communicative structure.

In the next chapter, we will immerse ourselves into every section, zooming through material gathered, and going into the details of how to structure and visualize the information on the slide.

CHAPTER 5

THE PROBLEM

Have you wondered why practically all the successful pitches that we've analyzed up 'til now start by describing a problem?

Remember the charts we saw in the previous chapter? The problem appeared very early on, and was present in practically all the analyzed pitches.

The only section equal to the problem in terms of noted presences was the solution, its alter ego.

By why do these two sections come before all the rest, and why are they so important?

5.1 GIVE THE PEOPLE WHAT THEY WANT

With S. Sinek, you have learned that people act selfishly. They are motivated by ideals that justify the actions, more than by the actions themselves. We are made as such, and we act to show the world that in which we believe.

"The people that worked with the Wright brothers for the construction of the first airplane were motivated by the same reason as the brothers. They knew that if they had been successful, their discovery could have changed the world forever.

Most of the collaborators worked on the project out of passion; the Wright brothers certainly did not have the possibility of financing a working team". [1]

Figure 1 - The first true airplane invented by the Wright brothers

Sinek emphasizes that these people had embraced the ideas of the Wright brothers and freely played a part in the project on their own, for something in which they believed, not to resolve a problem for the brothers.

Investors that listen to your pitch want to feel how you can resolve a problem that, for them, could have a notable business impact.

In some cases, the investors can be interested in financing start-ups that resolve problems that they perceive to be on a more personal level. This, in particular, is more frequently the case of the business anger, and less of the venture capitalist.

Thus, the desire of the audience is very clear. Your desire, on the other hand, is clearly that your idea is desirable, and that it be financed. For this, you need their attention during your presentation. But in order to have the attention of the audience, you must give something in exchange (Principle of Reciprocity, R. Cialdini).

With this, we can see the reason for commencing the pitch, by communicating to the audience the problem that you intend to resolve. You tell the people that you will resolve a problem they care about and, in exchange, ask for their attention to explain how you will do so.

Keep in mind that, if your audience is not interested in the problem, they certainly won't be interested in the rest of your presentation. In this case, however, there would not be anything else left to do, as it means you are talking to the wrong people.

Even within the same audience, there could people interested and others that are totally uninterested in your business. Make the problem immediately clear, and you will see that those who are interested will follow you. Do not be afraid to polarize your audience.

---

[1] Simon Sinek, How great leaders inspire action, ted.com

5.2 THE PROBLEM AS AN INTEGRAL PART OF STORYTELLING

With the application of the S.Co.R.E model of Dr Abela[2], we have given structure to an introduction based on the technique of storytelling.

Once the context (Situation) is defined, what arouses the interest is the problem (Complication), which the protagonist is forced to confront.

Thus, in a presentation designed to intrigue the audience through the use of a tale, the problem will naturally be placed in the first few slides.

Agrilyst – a platform of intelligent management of indoor farming – at the 2015 Techrunch Disrupt, won the day by this presentation:

"Hi, I'm Alice and this is Jason. We're the founders of Agrilyst, a platform that helps indoor cultivators to manage production. Agriculture is difficult; anyone that tries to cultivate tomatoes in the back garden knows what I'm talking about. Everything is trying to kill your plants: insects, too much sunlight, rain, even fawns.

So, what do you do if your business is the cultivation of food? You're going to waste a lot of time trying to limit the actions of all the factors that try to kill your plants, because this makes the difference between a successful business and a huge failure.

Figure 2 - Agrilyst Techrunch Disrupt 2015

[2] Abela A., The Presentation, CreateSpace Independent Publishing, 2010

For those that cultivate in a greenhouse, it isn't the slightest bit easier, as they have to worry about every little detail relative to the growth conditions, since controlling the growth conditions means controlling your profit.

Figure 3 - Agrilyst Techrunch Disrupt 2015

Tom, for example, is a greenhouse grower and manages 50,000 m² of surfaces cultivated every day. Tom loves to keep everything under control, and so has sensors that control the light, temperature, pH, humidity, etc. He wastes time by making notes by hand.

Figure 4 - Agrilyst Techrunch Disrupt 2015

But this is raw data, which can't be integrated into the business, and is thus useless for Tom. Therefore, Tom is going to lose hours looking through his notes to understand why something doesn't work the right way. He's going to invest to engage consultants to help him to identify eventual anomalies. Or, in the end, he's going to decide on the basis of his experience and his intuition every time a problem pops up.

Figure 5 - Agrilyst Techrunch Disrupt 2015

Tom's job doesn't necessarily have to be so difficult".[3]

Figure 6 - Agrilyst Techrunch Disrupt 2015

Alice starts the presentation by introducing the concept: agriculture is a difficult thing. Right from the start, she seeks to hook the audience in saying that all backyard tomato growers in the garden share the same problems as those a professional grower.

Then she arrives at her point and dispels the myth that growing in a greenhouse is simpler. She introduces a series of critiques and prepares the ground for a solution through a story. This deals with Tom, the grower that takes great pains to gather data from the greenhouse so as to interpret them quicker.

By starting from agriculture in general, she has succeeded in hooking the audience with problems that all of them are familiar with, or at least that which they have heard spoken. Only afterwards has she introduced the informational problems of the greenhouse, and she has done it through a story.

Do you see how the structure of the S.Co.R.E model appears again?

Situation: agriculture is difficult, and greenhouse cultivation has some specific problems. This is Tom's job and he manages a vast surface for cultivating daily.

Problem: unfortunately, however, Tom struggles because he has to deal with an enormous mass of formless data, and this costs him time and money.

From here onwards, we come in contact with the solution that we shall see in detail in the next chapter.

All in all, the images have succeeded in giving life to the story and have let Alice show the investors what she was talking about. We see then how slides play a crucial role in the presentation.

---

[3] Dillet R., And the winner of TechCrunch Disrupt SF 2015 is… Agrilyst, techcrunch.com

5.3 PROBLEM, PAIN, AND CONSEQUENCES

How do I introduce the problem that I seek to resolve, to people that, perhaps up 'til a few minutes before, didn't even know existed?

First of all, consider that, in the short time that you have, you cannot afford to be misunderstood, or even worse, not understood at all.

For this reason, independent of how involved you are in the more technical aspects of the business, it's fundamental to explain the problem in simple words, so that everyone may understand it.

Start by describing the inadequacy of the present solution. Here, it is simple (but not necessary) to tell a little story. When you describe the context (Situation, with reference to the Abela model of storytelling), it should come naturally to you to criticise the current situation.

If other solutions to the problem are present, and presently in use, you have already demonstrated that the solution exists and is relevant. The next problem is to show the limits of the currently-adopted solution. In doing so, you will have already led yourself toward the explanation of the competition.

In general, the current solutions could be slower, more expensive, and/or riskier. At this point, the audience could wonder which solution might resolve such problems the most effectively.

It seems clear that the speaker may have a solution in mind with which he is comparing the present alternatives, but what does he really have in mind?

Do you see how curiosity for the solution is generated? If you're able to trigger these dynamics in the minds of your listeners, it means that you have won their attention. When your solution brings an evident economic advantage, you have a golden opportunity to construct the problem on the present wastage.

If the client saves with your solution, the savings realised will be your market. We will see some examples ahead. For the moment, keep in mind that the problem, illustrated as a cost presently necessary, opens the way to a more efficient type of solution.

Furthermore, in showing the limits of the current solutions, you could take advantage of R. Caldini's technique of Contrast. Human beings are naturally drawn towards not letting an opportunity get away.

You know those discounts that the airlines or train companies email to you? Think about them for a second; maybe you didn't think about going home to your parents for the weekend; or maybe you didn't intend on going to see a friend of yours in another country. Then you get a 50% discount for a trip to go see your parents or to go see a friend. At that point, you are tempted to take it; you don't want to let go of the opportunity to travel at such a low price.

Obviously, because this technique works, you must be mindful of the original price. In this way, when you get the discount, you unconsciously make a comparison, you quantify just how cheap it is and you feel attracted by the offer.

Not too long ago, I developed a digital project that I sold through a dedicated site. On the landing page, there was a table of comparison of prices between the free versions and those with payment. Thus, I left open the possibility to test the software for free (with reduced functionality), or to buy it with all the functionalities at the full price.

If you decided to download the free version, you were sent to a page in which the download was confirmed, where you received a proposition of a 50% discount if you bought it immediately, before closing the page.

This technique took advantage of the fact that the user had perceived the value of the product at the full price on the landing page in which he was presented with all the characteristics.

In the moment in which the offer was presented, it was clearly an opportunity and this motivated the users towards the purchase.

An example of this technique applied to an investor pitch? One of my favourite pitches, Airbnb!

Figure 7 - The problem of how to compare with the solution presently available

Look at the slide of the problem that I have highlighted. Let's try to imagine the discussion together:

"When you travel, has it ever occurred that you get prices from hotels that are way too high, in hotels way too far from the local culture and in places where you can't even book a room with people from the area or even let you have travelers as guests? […]"

Do you feel the growing curiosity? While you listen to the discussion, you understand that the speaker is about to hit you with a solution to the problem, and you grow more impatient to hear it.

At this point, the pitch of Airbnb already proposes the solution. If you want to strengthen the effect and grow the expectation, you could deepen the pain by detailing the consequences for the travelers.

"Example: If you are like me, when you return home after a journey, you've spent much more money than you thought you would, you've not really seen neither the place, nor the local culture. You know that sense of frustration, of disappointment? […]".

With this little addition, I'm entering into the emotional sphere by recalling frustration and disappointment as displeasing sensations for the listener.

Moreover, I have placed myself into the story, creating a connection with the audience on the basis of a common experience. Having lived this pain myself, I understand it and therefore become more credible in the eyes of the audience.

Thus, if you think about it, the instinct to resolve problems is drawn in the DNA of the human race. We are used to eating if we feel hungry, to cover ourselves if we feel cold, etc.

All in all, we are born to be problem solvers. So we are naturally attracted to a communicative structure that contemplates the usage of a dynamic problem/solution.

5.4 WHEN THE PROBLEM DOESN'T EXIST YET

In some cases, the problem could be not clearly identified. If you've patented an innovative bicycle that can't be stolen, the problem is clearly the theft of the bike; if you've invented a solution that reduces the costs for the greenhouse farmer and gathers all the necessary data to facilitate the management of his work, it is quite intuitive to understand that the present situation will show the easily identifiable inefficiencies as problems.

However, some innovations are such that their problems are not yet evident on the market. These are innovations that are justified by attentive observation of trends.

Think about the launch of the iPhone. No one could have asked for a device that unites computer, mp3 player and telephone.

Here's how Steve Jobs responded to the questions posed to him during the 2003 Digital Conference (D1). [4]

Interviewer: *In your opinion, what is the present state of the evolution of the cell phone, of the PC and of the internet?*

S.J.: *The personal computer is an extraordinary thing and has evolved from an obvious instrument to something more [...]. With the invention of the spreadsheet, the PC has passed from personal use to much more professional. [...] Then the internet arrived. People started to buy more powerful PCs, that could hold faster web browsers [...].*
At Apple, we believe that the PC is entering into a new stage, the third stage. The PC is becoming a truly digital hub. How many of you have a digital camera? (The audience raise their hands). Your camera can't do anything without a personal computer that saves the pictures and shows them to you. The PC is becoming the container of your photos, of your information, of your music [...].

Steve Jobs demonstrated himself to be very convinced in the explanation of the first trend, the PC that became a more and more complete machine, a true multimedia centre for every kind of use, from the personal sphere to the professional one.

Interviewer: *Couldn't the iPod have an internet connection and replace the PC?*

S.J.: *It could, but the PC has a proper large hard drive, a big screen, a big keyboard, excellent internet, with processes that support powerful applications. You couldn't have a true music shop in your pocket, unless a foldable display were invented that would allow you to access your music comfortably [...]".*

Interviewer: *What do you think of a PDA? Couldn't the iPod integrate its functionalities one day?*

S.J.: *[...] of all the people in the world that use PDA, 90% of them want to read information, and 10% only want to insert information. People only want a deposit of their information, and where they can rarely insert a new telephone number.*

At Apple, we believe that the phone will let go of this role. Looking at the trends, it's clear that the cell phone market is exploding, everyone will have a phone in their own pocket[...].

On one hand, Jobs shows the discomfort of having to consult a music store on the screen of the iPod, because it's too small. On the other hand, he highlights that the cell phone market is growing and that one day the cell phones will take the places of PDAs.

This interview is quite old, but it still has a lot to teach us. Looking at the interview in its entirety—and I encourage you to do so—it seems like Jobs is already speaking of the iPhone, that didn't exist at that time.

---

[4] Steve Jobs in 2003 at D1 the First D All Things Digital Conference, youtube.com

Jobs was a visionary, he had a profound understanding of his consumers. During the whole interview, he affirms with assuredness what people look for and speaks of how people will act in future.

Hearing him speak about the conclusion of creating a device that integrates telephone, music and internet seems obvious! Incredible.

So for all the start-ups that are that innovative, that don't resolve a present problem but operate in the future and base their entrepreneurial vision on assumptions of evolutions of some trends of the market, my advice is that of introducing the presentation by speaking exactly about these trends. Imagine the pitch in the case of Jobs we just saw:

• Most people use PDA for the extraction of information (reading is easier that writing on these devices).

• So people need a device that stores information that can be consulted on the go.

• In the meantime, the cell phone market is visibly growing and, before long, we will all have a phone in our pocket.

• The future is merely waiting for a phone that can also store all our information and provide them to us comfortably every time we need it.

• I present to you the iPhone, a revolutionary phone, a touch screen mp3 player, and innovative device for internet communication.

Obviously, this is a restrictive example, because in the launch of the iPhone, other trends were included in it, such as listening to music and internet navigation. However, this simple example lets us comprehend the approach of the start-up presentations that aren't created to resolve an existing problem, but rather to anticipate a future trend.

5.5 PERSUASION APPLIED TO THE PROBLEM

In chapter 3, we defined together the three pillars at the basis of persuasive communication: credibility, focus on the audience, emotion.

Let's see how these three principles are applied to the description of a problem.

5.5.1 Credibility

When you develop a business activity on the basis of a problem, it is fundamental that your connection with the problem is strong, or at least that you are aware of it.

Who do you think would invest in you, knowing that you are seeking to resolve a problem that you know nothing about? First of all, when you introduce the problem, try to be clear. Speak with a comprehensible language, as if you were speaking to a child.

Let's dispel the myth that speaking with big words shows competence. If you wish to be credible, speak to your investor in a comprehensible way and show yourself as sure of your profound knowledge of the problem you seek to resolve.

This is why, for example, it is important to show that in the team, there are members whose previous experiences might bring the subjects to know the problems and its facets. In the third chapter, we said that, according to Professor J. A. Conger, the credibility of a speaker is based on two principal factors:

- The knowledge of the subject
- His relationships

For this reason, oftentimes initial stories are very effective when the speaker presents a personal story that connects him directly to the problem.

On the Uber website, the first few lines tell us that in 2008, Travis Kalanicj and Garrent Camp found themselves in difficulty in Paris trying to find a taxi, from where came the idea of booking a driver with a simple tap.

Figure 8 - The story of Uber

If you yourself have suffered the pain of that problem, so much so that you felt the need to resolve it, it means you understand it and you understand the market.

I have recently supported start-ups in the field of a program in biology and medicine. It was a delicate invention, 3D radiography, creating innovative probiotics in the formulation of machines that simulate the human heart. In most of these start-ups, the team was composed of doctors, biomedical engineers or other employees. I remember in particular one start-up that presented an innovative tub for assisted immersive birth, the founder of which was Austrian.

Another pitch I found myself working on in this period, for example, regards a start-up that wants to spread information to stimulate the prevention of cancer. The founder was herself a cancer survivor.

You know that she knows what she's talking about, because she has lived it in first person.

In these cases, your listener doesn't struggle to believe you, because he knows that the problem of which you speak and that you are seeking to resolve, is one you know very well directly. If you understand the problem, it means that you understand that which should touch your potential clients.

The comprehension of your potential clients is fundamental for the success of the business. Each sales strategy, marketing strategy and every attempt to reach the market objective with your product/service, will be just as effective as your comprehension of the needs of these people.

If you don't have a direct relationship with the problem, you could connect yourself to it through a person close to you. For example, in the TED of Jorge Soto, "The future of early cancer detection", analyzed earlier, he speaks of a problem lived by his aunty (See the transcription in section 2.3.)

Here is the application of the second principle of Professor J. A. Conger, based on relationships.

Finally, if you don't have direct experience and your relationships don't help you, you can only turn to authoritative sources or to experts of the sector.
The first case, for example, is typical in circumstances in which you speak of trends. As long as you are not known as a trustworthy visionary, when you show trends and take advantage of them to introduce your solution, it is important that the trends are drawn from reliable sources.

As you can see, you could avail yourselves with the documentation and study the problem at the heart in order to then use the solid sources and illustrate it.
The case in which you avail yourself of experts of the sector or external consultants is a bit like returning to the point of the relationships. All in all, if you do not have them, you can always construct them, or, at worst, pay for them.

5.5.2 Focus on the audience

We have seen that people act purely for their own benefit and so investors act in order to realise an investment that might have an interesting economic return.

How do you then render your problem or that of someone close to you so interesting for an investor, that he's convinced to finance your entrepreneurial activity?

Assuming that you have convinced the investor of the fact that your problem exists (credibility), now you must make another step and you must demonstrate that the problems generate an important impact in economic terms: if many people suffer the same problem and today pay to resolve it, it is interesting. Alternatively, they could not pay yet, but be disposed to do so if there were a possible solution.

Now it is up to you to demonstrate that people suffer the problem, so much so that they are disposed to pay to resolve it. At the moment, there is not even talk of solution, as it isn't a question of how unique and significant the solution might be, but rather how painful the problem is for people today.

Some time ago, I followed a start-up that created an intelligent central unit that optimizes the energy consumption of buildings. In their pitch, they showed me a slide in which, through a bar chart, they show the monthly consumption in the present case, and then how the height of the bars is reduced when the control unit is switched on.

While the intervention of the control unit forms part of the solution, showing the bars with the present consumption allows them to affirm that today people already spend enormous amounts to have a certain service. In this case, a provider of electricity.

You must understand that, as we saw when we spoke of solutions that make savings, the problem has paved the way towards the solution that will have a strong convincing effect on the audience of investors.

The message is very simple: tomorrow I will make you spend less for something for which today you spend more. Who wouldn't want it?

So your idea is able to generate an economic advantage for a certain kind of client. If between the advantage and the present expenditure a margin of earnings for you can be drawn out, the investor will immediately straighten his antennae towards your profitable business.

Always remember that the investors are not interested in your idea, no more than they are interested in your specific problem. The investors are interested in your idea as a means of resolving a problem that can generate earnings for them. For this reason, it is fundamental to bring down the problem to terms comprehensible to your audience, whether they are investors or potential strategic partners.

In some situations, you could find yourself having to divide the process of persuasion into different parts. In fact, it is often necessary to explain the relevance of the problem for the potential clients of your start-up and successively express the business potential of the present unresolved problem.

Let's imagine that you have invented software that allows the automatic update of servers for big server farms.
You could introduce it by saying (the numbers are invented):

In the world. there are a hundred thousand server farms that update their servers daily. The server updates require dedicated, qualified staff, who work for long hours and are subject to human errors. With our software, the server farms will update automatically, rapidly and without getting the servers wrong, from now and for always!

As you can see, I have introduced the context and then I have explained the problem which the server farms have to confront. Up 'til now, I have given a motive for the existence of the problem, but this is not enough, because the investors may not be interested. So, I proceed by saying:

"A qualified technician today costs one hundred thousand Euros a year, on average, to a server farm, and at least five of them are needed to guarantee the operability of a server farm of average dimensions. Furthermore, it is estimated that, because of human errors and slow intervention times tied to the manuality of the operations of maintenance, the farms lose five hundred thousand Euros a year. All in all, between the staff and the wastage due to the errors today, an average server farm loses about a million Euros a year".

Here is how it becomes immediately interesting for the investors. Where there is a possibility of optimization and a client that reasonably wishes to save, there is also an excellent market for a solution that works.

At this point the doubt in the mind of the investor could be, *"Maybe the solution that he's proposing isn't able to realize this optimization."*

Congratulations! You have succeeded in hooking the investor and making him curious about your solution.

5.5.3 Emotionality

Emotions influence our ability to make decisions. A famous neuroscientist, Antonio Damasio, conducted an important study on people that had experienced damage to the part of the brain that generates emotions.[5]

---

[5] Damasio A., Emotion, decision making and the orbitofrontal cortex, 2000

Damasio demonstrated that people without emotions were unable to make even very simple decisions, like selecting between one plate and another for dinner.

When we present, we tend to always provide all the rational motivations that we believe are necessary for the audience to decide to accept and adopt our ideas, but the truth is that people act because they want to, more than because it rationally suits them.

When we present the problem, it's not helpful to tell people what is right and what is wrong. It ends up being much more efficient to guide the audience towards the discovery of what they could want. Here, we return to the theme of the mentor that guides the audience (the true protagonist of every presentation).

For this reason, the negotiators work a lot by listening and seek to identify the deep problem that motivates the listener, so as to adapt the solutions and persuade them to act.
In our case, we can save one stem. We don't need to ask the investors what problem they seek to resolve—we already know.
Investors want to realize the maximum earnings possible by risking as little as possible.

How do we present the problem in such a way as to stimulate the audience and convince them to listen to your solution?

We need to create an attack based on a story that is the most efficient possible. We have already seen that to create an efficient story, it is fundamental to create a point of reference between the audience and the story.

In 2009, Bill Gates spoke of eradicating malaria in a famous TED talk[6]:

[6] Gates B., Mosquitos, malaria and education, TED, 2009, ted.com

"[...]For example, more money is invested in baldness preventing medicine than in anti-malarial medicine. Sure, baldness is terrible... (laughter) And overall, rich people are bald. This is what established the priority.

But even the huge numbers of a million people killed every year by malaria should not lead us to greatly underestimate its impact.

Every moment, 200 million people suffer from it. This means that economies in these zones cannot develop, because its slowing effect is very powerful.

Malaria is certainly transmitted by mosquitoes".

Figure 9 - B. Gates, Mosquitoes, malaria and education, TED, 2009

"I've brought some of them here, so that you try them as well. We'll let them buzz around the auditorium for a bit. (Laughter). There's no reason why this privilege must be reserved to the poor. (Laughter) (Applause) [...]."

Bill Gates speaks of malaria to an audience that, very probably, perceives it as a problem very far from reality. For this reason, at a certain point, he opens the bowl with some mosquitoes and frees them, rendering a far problem very close, that of all taking advantage of fear.
If you're wondering, the mosquitoes had no effect, but the pretence was enough to hook the attention of the audience and make them curious of the solution that Bill proposed.

5.6 Summarizing

People act egoistically, for pure personal interest. So always start your presentation by speaking of the problem that you intend on resolving.

Be credible and present a significant problem to your listener. Insert the problem within your story that levers on the emotions of the audience. Remember, emotion determines how people make decisions.

If you catch the audience with an interesting problem, you have opened the way to interest, to present your solution and strike the investors.

CHAPTER 6

THE SOLUTION

As we covered in chapter 4, all presentations have the binomial problem/solution at the beginning.
If you introduce the problem in an effective way, you project yourself towards the solution. Show that your solution is up to the problem, that it will solve it, and that it will be unique with regards to the other solutions available on the market.

6.1 UNIQUE VALUE PROPOSITION

With the introduction of the problem, you create suspense. If you complete this task effectively, you'll bring the audience to its maximum level of curiosity, and they will be ready to know more about your idea.

Imagine the problem as going uphill a roller coaster. Amongst the problem and the solution, there is a peak moment before the great descent.

The descent is normally something sensational, something that will take the breath away and will leave your audience with an emotional, unforgettable memory. If you think deeply about that, it is the descent, in fact, that motivates the uphill climb.

The same thing is true for the solution. Don't kill the faint of heart in your audience, but aim for an epical beginning, because this is the moment you will imprint in the memory of your potential investors.

Do you remember the Agrylist example from the previous chapter? The ending of the problem stated this way:

"Tom will waste many hours looking through the notes, in order to understand what is not working properly. He will invest by employing consultants that may be able to help him to identify possible anomalies. Or he will finally decide, on the basis of his own experience and intuition, every time a problem arises.

Tom's work is not that difficult. With Agrylist, all of Tom's data communicates amongst his devices, eliminating the need to make decisions based on intuition".

Figure 1 - Agrylist UVP

After illustrating the problem, the above quote explains clearly and in a concise manner what Agrylist is, in one simple sentence. Thanks to this simple and powerful definition, the presenter, Alison, has linked the solution to the problem, and defined, her start up in an unmistakable manner start-up.

Triangle, objective-explaining sentence is called a "unique value proposition" (UVP), and is valuable to anyone seeking fast information on your start-up.

"Your UVP is simply who you are as a company. This is your Inside Reality. It's your personality, your identity, and your strengths. A UVP tells you and your team what you are all about".[1]

 An UVP, in theory, should explain the point of your business, while answering three questions:[2]

1. Which clients?
2. Which need?
3. At which price?

[1] Onlinemarketinggiant.com
[2] Unique value proposition, isc.hbs.edu

Figure 2 - The three UVP questions

The client will typically be a part of the story you have exploited to introduce the problem. In fact, Alison introduces the solution by making reference to her character Tom. Alison covers the first two questions in her UVP, but did not cover the price.

Do you remember Marcela Sapone's speech when she introduced Alfred's pitch? Marcela has been more educational because she introduced the price as well.

"[…] Dan needs help, Dan needs Alfred!"

Figure 3 - Introduction to solution

"Finally the luxury of a customized service for any of us. For $99/month, Dan can have a personal Alfred every week to take care of his home chores".

Which is the best solution among the two, in your opinion? Educationally, the second one is more complete, but I personally believe that the most important thing, when you are introducing your UVP, is for it to be short and extremely concise.

I do not believe the price to be essential at this stage, as further into the pitch, we will talk about business models. However, it is critical to answer the other two questions: for whom, and which need?

Therefore, the UVP is your solution shown in a short and concise manner, following the presentation of the problem. Finally, this is the connection point between the problem and the solution.

There is another technique start-up used to explain the start up's existence: the cross-sector comparison with another well-known company.

Here some examples:
• We assess professionals, we are people TripAdvisors
• We allow you to lease your garage on a daily basis, we are the Airbnb of private car parks

This technique, in my opinion, is messing communication a bit and risks of making you lose originality, but can have a sensational communication impact, because it quickly makes the concept clear.

This is the reason you should never use it as a replacement of UVP. Therefore, if you have a valid comparison on which to lean in order to clarify what you are doing, use it after having communicated your UVP.

6.2 DEMO: SHALL I DO IT OR NOT?

In my opinion, yes, but with some caution. The demo represents the moment when you show your product to the audience.

There are various methods through which we can show the product/service we are offering. Usually, when the product is already operational, we tend to do the so-called live demonstration. In the case of digital products—apps, Internet websites, etc—it often takes the form of a speaker-guided tour through a shared screen session.

Showing your product in action to the audience is one of the most effective marketing tools you can utilize. After all, seeing is believing.

However, pay attention to any unexpected circumstances. Always keep in mind that when presenting, you will be nervous and excited about your product, and very much focused on what you have to say. Add to this the technical problems caused by PowerPoint, Keynote, by the on-board technician, by the presentation screen, etc. and you have the makings of a great disappointment.

In short, the day the unforeseeable circumstance happens, everything could be instantly lost. Imagine, for instance, that you want to show your new Internet website live. What would happen if the wi-fi connection becomes defective? What would happen if the connection is lost because too many users are already connected to the network? These are trivial but extremely concrete examples of unforeseeable circumstances that are quite possible, and much more common than you could imagine.

In 2010, Steve Jobs introduced the iPhone 4, and at the moment of the live demo, things didn't go the way he and his investors expected. The iPhone that Jobs wanted to use to show a video call wasn't able to connect to the network.

Only twenty minutes later, Jobs confirmed that his technician solved the problem, and that the real cause was that too many devices were connected simultaneously to the same wi-fi network.

A recent example occurred a few months ago, when a start-up that wanted to use Prezi for his presentation, despite the founder having given notice, he was requested to use a safe PowerPoint, accompanied by PDF.

The day of the pitch, for some technical reason, the presentation in Prezi did not work and so the team found itself in the situation of having to completely redo the presentation, bringing it back to a PowerPoint document.

Imagine the nerves of that team when they discovered the problem. After something like this happens, you would no longer be bright and ready to go for a brilliant presentation, risking your presentation out of a trivial technical problem.

Let me invite you to take a look to Seenit pitch, which, in 2016, won the Start-up Battlefield of London Disrupt[3]. At one point, the presenter launched a video, but unfortunately, no audio was heard. For about 30 seconds, the situation remained the same until a colleague found the solution and relaunched the video. Meanwhile, the founder asked the staff if the timer was running, in order to decide if it was necessary to show the video. In this case, luckily, the timer was stopped and after half a minute, the video started again with the audio.

What would have happened if the director had not decided to stop the timer? A pitch presentation is already a short, sharp affair. If part of your short time is wasted solving some technical problem, the risk of failure increases significantly.

---

[3] Seenit wins Startup Battlefield at Disrupt London 2016, techcrunch.com

Sometimes even a simple live video can be risky. From what I have said until now, it may seem my aim is to discourage to use a demo, but that is not that case. In fact, I recommend showing your product, but my advice is not to show it live. Use screen capture applications, or some small videos that would allow the audience to view how your idea works.

If your product hasn't been developed yet, use some mock ups. If it is a physical product, you could show some composite photographs, with your product placed in context.

Show your product with no hesitation, but avoid live demonstrations in real time.

Finally, always execute your demo as if you were a real customer using your product. This will make your execution even more concrete, connecting it to the previous story, where you use a character to tell the story, and it will make it that much easier for the audience to live that experience.

In fact, people tend to empathize with the main character of the story, and so become part of the story themselves.

Reconnect yourself to the story you used in order to relate the problem, and show how to solve it through the main character using your solution.

6.3 THE SOLUTION AS SAVING

One of the main problems of the start-up early stage is that often the idea living in the mind of the founder is very far from the real dynamics of the market.

We will later see what challenges rise when it comes to implementing an idea, even compared to other products of the same form. The truth is that often the product with a concrete base and form won't find any significant match on the market.

Consumers may not buy it, or they do not want to pay for it—or even worse, it is no longer something that gains a lot of interest. Let's suppose that the solution would interest the consumer, you will still need to ensure that the business model and price don't scare off investors and customers.

You could propose a freemium model to distribute as a demo or a test version, then encouraging customers towards the paid premium option; you could have a periodic subscription model; or simply apply a one-off price, etc.

There is the option for various business models, but we will talk about that in another section. For the time being, you should keep the problem of the price/value balance in mind. It is possible that when you enter the market with your idea, the answer will be negative or, more likely, unexpected.

In my previous entrepreneurial adventure, I was taking care of a start-up marketing that was forming a platform where, amongst other things, the ski instructors could collect feedback from their customers. In short, some kind of LinkedIn for sport instructors.

This idea garnered great interest on the market, and the ski schools were looking forward to its launch. For this reason, we decided to let customers test the product for a few months, and then introduce a low monthly fee.

When we started talking about a fee, customers started to complain and to close down their pages. One of the most frequent critiques was, "If I got Facebook for free, why should I pay you?".

While the customer's excuse was weak at best, this was highlighting a perception problem of the brand, but was forcing us into discussing the way we thought our business should be run at the time.

The same solution offered to the hotels instead got the opposite effect, simply because the hotels were already used to paying much more for Tripadvisor or Booking. So a similar solution for a price well below the competition's bench marks would immediately strike them as interesting.

It all consists of understanding what, if anything, the client is already paying for, in order to solve his problem. If he is already paying, this means that the problem is a big issue for his business, and if your product helps him save with a similar solution, the client would jump on your product.

6.4 PERSUASION APPLIED TO THE SOLUTION

In Steve Blank's[4] pyramid, the first two steps in a start-up life cycle are related to the binomial problem-solution.

In my opinion, this is the start-up Bermuda triangle, a place where they enter, but hardly ever emerge alive.

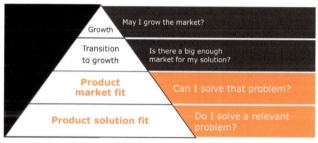

Figure 4 - Start-up pyramid, S. Blank

> "Customer Validation proves that you have found a set of customers and a market who react positively to the product, by relieving those customers of some of their money..."
>
> **Steve Blank**[5]

If the first question for a start-up to ask is related to the significance of the problem to solve, the second one relates to their own capacity to really solve the problem.

In this chapter, you have learned to introduce the solution, following a well specified order of topics, but would you believe it will be convincing for the investors?

[4] Blank S., The Four Steps to the Epiphany, K&S Ranchn, 2013
[5] Ellis S., The startup pyramid, startup-marketing.com

If the investors won't be completely convinced about your capacity to override even just the second step of the pyramid, it won't be easy to collect all the funding.
How do you convince the investors to believe in your capacity to successfully deliver the right solution?

6.4.1 Credibility

The first aspect to work on is your own credibility. If you identify a serious problem and then you are not able to solve it, you won't be credible.

However, the fact that you really would be able to solve it won't automatically make you credible. It will be important that you follow the advice coming from persuasion sciences, in order to convince the investors.

According to Jay A., there are two aspects to the basis of credibility:
1. The knowledge of the topic
2. Its relationships

During a consultancy project on an investor pitch I provided support to a start-up operating in public administration, thanks to my team.

The team created a solution to optimize municipal expenses, creating a network of shared resources that could be exchanged between Municipals, which could be spent on the platform.

A solution for this problem is obvious. In your opinion, if the Italian Municipals could pay less for a better product, would that be a good solution?

It is best to understand the relevance and truthfulness of the problem. So let's validate the first step of the pyramid. You need to deeply understand how you want to solve the problem in order to do so.

A solution for an issue with the Italian public administration is to be gained by being skeptical. I am not an expert in the field. However, when I think of a public administration, some concepts come to my mind: bureaucracy, slowness, paperwork, complexity, and low levels of innovation.

In such a context, I can imagine that a start-up won't have an easy life.

I asked the team to explain what their references would be, and why they believed they would be able to solve the problem.

From there, I discovered that one of the founding members was a lawyer already operating inside the municipal system, while the other two owned a very important company that was providing services to a good number of municipals on the national territory.

The first member, since he was a municipal employee, provided the knowledge and deep understanding of the topic. Who better than a person on the inside could know these dynamics?

The other two were stronger on the relationships topic, having developed supply relationships with municipals all over the country in the course of their history.

Moreover, the other two already had a successful entrepreneurial history behind them, and this was reinforcing their credibility. In fact, one of the main causes for start-up bankruptcy is the team's lack of experience.

In this case, the investors could never have put the discussion into a team capacity, in order to develop an idea that would sell to the public administration world.

I once came across a start-up that I was trying to make smart tables, for use in restaurants. I won't get into the merits of the technology, but it is sufficient to say that they wanted to develop a device that would connect all the tables of the restaurant, and other great things.

At the question related to the go-to market, the team faltered. An investor asked, *"How do you believe you will spread this device to the restaurants in the territory?"*

One of the founders answered, *"Easy! First of all, we get the huge fast food chains, then we will sell it to McDonalds, Burger King and others like them. We will soon generate big numbers with few customers".*

This plan seemed to be impeccable, but then arrived the decisive question. *"Have you ever sold to a fast food chain, or do you have any contacts that make you hopeful you would at least be able to meet the right guys?"*

The founder was completely surprised and answered, *"Actually, no, for both cases. We thought we would get in touch with someone inside the organization using LinkedIn".*

Now, don't get me wrong, I am not saying that using LinkedIn to approach potential customers is wrong, I am just underlining the total lack of experience and connection network of the founder.

As you can guess, the weakness of the two main pillars of persuasion would make the team seem less credible, and dampen its ability to create a solution.

Would you invest in a team that is basing its success on the sale to customers to whom they have never sold anything, and who do not know the organizational dynamics of the sector? I don't think so.

6.4.2 Focus on the audience

Quoting C. Lipp, start-up pitch coach at Standford University, *"When Steve Jobs introduced the iPod in 2001, he said that the iPod had 20 minutes of 'skip protection' [functionality], so that it wouldn't even lose a fragment of a song during 'training' [consumer benefit]. If Steve Jobs had presented it to the investors, he could have added that since people can use the iPod during their training, the market of potential consumers interested in this product would be greater [investor benefit]"*.[6]

Lipp is talking about the difference between consumer benefit and investor benefit. When you are presenting a solution, it would be more effective to speak from the standpoint of the consumer whose problem is being solved, thanks to the use of the service/product offered by the start-up.

In fact, in the initial story, it is common use to employ a character that would represent the typical consumer. The consequence is that the solution will be introduced with a focus on the benefits for the consumer.

Although this would be a great approach for a sales presentation to the end consumer, in an investor pitch, we should make an additional step, suggests Lipp. In fact, there will be the need to transform the benefit for the consumer into a benefit for the investor.

In the iPod example, Chris did hypothesise that Steve Jobs could have made the additional step towards the investors, highlighting the strategic and business reasons behind the choice to introduce an additional functionality for the consumers.

Always remember that the solution is developed for the customer but an investor pitch is talking to the investors.

[6] Lipp C., The startup pitch, 2014

You have the responsibility to set the communication so that it would seem interesting and hopefully convincing at the investors' eyes.

6.4.3 Emotionality

The successful pitch investors are always looking for are introduced by an initial storytelling that would allow, if created well, to reduce the audience's waning attention and bring them back to focus on the product.

Usually, the story is based upon a character that can be the founder or a consumer (real or invented), who is experiencing the problem.

A great speaker connects, directly or indirectly, to the character, and exploits him as a connection bridge with the audience. In fact, even if the speaker hasn't lived the story directly, the speaker could state that they know the main character, and so raise their credibility.

The people that listen to a story have the tendency to empathize with the main character, and emotionally experience the pain caused by the problem.

With the introduction of the solution, the main character will feel relieved and will show the benefits of the product (benefit for the consumer or unique selling proposition). Therefore, the audience will feel the same relief as the character when the problem is solved.

Moreover, the audience feeling part of the story and living the connection with the character, is more likely to seek out the same solution. If the speaker correctly connected, he will indirectly gain the trust of the audience.

In short, telling the story of a consumer that is living the problem and is using your solution conquers the audience, and will gain you the trust of the listener.

Therefore, emotion in the solution is strictly related to the capacity to build an effective story, starting from the problem.

The solution is an integral part of introductory storytelling (see S.Co.R.E. model of Dr. Abela).

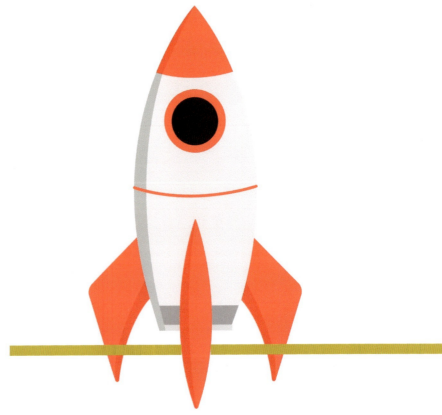

6.5 Summarizing

Introduce the solution in a clear and concise manner, identifying it as your Unique Value Proposition, and presenting the materials that support the solution. Build up a demo, from the end user's standpoint, that shows your product is working and, more specifically, how to solve the proposed problem.

Remember to avoid live demonstrations. To avoid all possible unforeseeable circumstances, use the screen capture feature or small, pre-recorded videos.

If you have audio, verify that it can be properly heard in the back section of the hall before starting the presentation. If something goes wrong, once you are presenting, this will force you to stop. I believe, it will always be better to waste a few minutes at the beginning of your presentation in order to be sure that everything is working properly and ensure a presentation with no hindrances. Use the presentation persuasion techniques analysed to convince the audience, creating authoritativeness and credibility. Communicate with the audience using language, tune with those that are listening to you, excite them, and become memorable.

CHAPTER 7

MARKET SIZE

Alright, let's suppose you have convinced the investors in the audience about the strategic value of your problem, and about the validity of your solution. You have done quite a good job, but that is not enough.

The investor, as we have seen, is now reasoning in terms of profit and will evaluate your business project as an investment opportunity.

> *"I like opportunities that target markets that are so huge that even the management team is struggling to thoroughly understand"*
>
> Don Valentine, Sequoia Capital[1]

Moreover, the professional investor that is dealing with a start-up, either a business angel or an investment fund, is looking for investments with a high rate of return, and thus with big ambition projects.

If you want the investor to make a step forward towards his decision to finance your project, you have to show that you are operating in an interesting market. The solution you are proposing should at least have the potential—in theory—to generate the revenues that you and the investor desire so much.

The market size is therefore the size of the total amount spent inside a certain sector by a specific target of consumers. It is not what is spent for your services/products, but the total amount spent, including that spent on your competitors.

Alfred, start-up winner of the Techrunch Disrupt 2014, ascertains the market size this way:

> **Marcela Sapone:**
>
> *"There are 18 million home owners in the first 10 towns that have this service, and are already paying more than €227 billion for the home services on which Alfred relies. The on-demand services are spreading all over the world and, where on-demand home services are available, we represent the natura consequence"*

Figure 1 - Market size, pitch Alfred, Techrunch Disrupt 2014

How do you determine the market in order to make it seem interesting to the eyes of a professional investor? How do you show business ambition behind some simple charts, and attract the best investments?

[1] Francisco S. Homem de Mello, Hacking the Startup Investor Pitch: What Sequoia Capital's business plan framework can teach you about building and pitching your company, Ajax Books, 2014

7.1 PREDICTING THE FUTURE LOOKING AT THE TRENDS?

Being able to study our own market means also being able to portray its dynamics. Understanding the market's operational logics will allow you to make assumptions on its future development.

For this reason, it will be extremely important to study and monitor the trends. Remember the example of the 2003 digital conference, where Steve Jobs was answering questions on the market development based upon his analysis of the trends at that time?

I find it amazing how Steve Jobs already had clear what would have happened in the following ten years. Listening him talking, it would almost seem that he was in our times… a little over ten years ago!

A mentor once told me that in order to create a start-up, you should have the future in your mind. He maintained that realizing something that would be innovative today would mean being confident enough to realize something that is innovative tomorrow would already be out of date. If you really want to innovate, you should create something that would still be innovative in ten years' time.
Studying the trends can show you the direction the market is taking.

For example, *Buffer* paints the social media scene as it talks about what is happening.
There are more than 200 million tweets every day, and more than a half of them contains links. Four million pieces of content are posted on Facebook every day. Zuckerberg's law shows an exponential growth of the shares and the traffic coming from social media will soon pass the one coming from search engines.

Here, a tool like Buffer, which is used to plan sharing content on various social networks, positions itself on a dynamic, high-growth market. Therefore, it would in fact be topical, but has a potentially-explosive future.

Social Media Landscape

- Of 200M daily Tweets, 55% contain links
- 4 billion items shared on Facebook per day
- Zuckerberg's Law shows exponential growth of sharing
- Traffic through social is soon to surpass traffic from search

Figure 2 - Social media trend analysis from Buffer pitch

Considering that an investor will invest in a start-up in view of future profits, the bigger the growth potential of the market where the start-up fits into, the lesser the risk to invest into a product that would become obsolete before it's finished.

Generally, assigning our own product/service to a positive trend could also result in opportunities that you could access otherwise.

I remember one experience I had in an investment fund where, many years ago, its CEO sensed the explosive growth of cryptocurrencies. So the whole team started studying to understand that world, and in few months, we built a new investment vehicle to finance start-ups that would operate in that sector.

We paid great attention not to letting any business opportunity operating on that market slip away. We engaged with some trends that we believed in, and this automatically gave value to the start-up that were operating.

7.2 FROM POTENTIAL TO SERVED MARKET

Here is a simple and effective model to determine the market you can add into a pitch presentation for the investors.

TAM (Total Available Market): the total market that includes the overall expenditure in a certain sector.

For example, if we think of the computers world, the overall market will include personal computers, laptops, notebooks and so on.

When you hear people talking about the market determination, they are generally referring to the TAM.

SAM (Served Available Market): served market corresponds to that part you would like to achieve with your product service.

In reference to the computers market, for instance, you may want to compete on the laptop market, and eliminate other markets.

SOM (Share of Market): the market share corresponding to the SAM percentage you expect to get.

Figure 3 - TAM, SAM, SOM

Where will you locate these figures for your specific case?

Extensive research on the Internet represents an excellent road to travel on. Let me warn you, however, not to get lost into countless figures coming from the countless reports you will find online.

When you start searching, you will soon realize that you will never locate figures ready for use, updated to the current year. You will then have to combine various sources, maybe with data that has not been updated at the same time.

In many cases, you could even find specific figures and will so have to determine them bottom up.

Let's make an example: how many laptops are sold in the town of Milan? You may not find such a detail online.

In this case, you could determine the market by counting how many families live in Milan (a datum that can for sure be found with an excellent approximation), establish the average number of laptops for family, and you are all set!

What happens if the figures are not accurate?

The market determination is obviously an estimate. It can be more accurate, and is certainly based upon more reliable sources, but will always remain an estimate.

For this reason, do not worry about having accurate figures, because it will be almost impossible and because the investors are used to estimating the markets size they are investing in. The important thing is that, through reliable sources, you will be able to present a quite interesting market that would justify the required investment.

7.3 BE AMBITIOUS AND FORGET THE VC

The VC needs to identify those start-ups that could increase his investment ten times over in a relatively short time frame (3-5 years).

This will allow the venture capital funds to be sustainable, and thus to be able to pay back their investors.
For this reason, a VC won't invest in any start-up that would not have the adequate potential to create such multiple earnings.

Let's take a simple example:

Let's say that a VC would fund your start-up for €200k and that you would become a partner holding 10%. This will mean that your start-up has been valued €2M (€200k /10%).

Years after, you have been able to conquer that famous 1% of market share. On exit day, your start-up has an annual turnover of €1M and is valued at €3M. So the market today is worth €100M. You then decide to sell your investment fund and settle his 10%.

The fund will get €300k from the sale of shares, having realized €100k in profits. We can certainly say that it has not been liable for a loss, however, the outcome is quite far from the x10 it should have created investing in your start-up.

Considering that these balances are based on a €100M market, that could appear huge, if valued in absolute terms, but if you think about it, downstream from such calculations, you will understand how much you should aim aloft in order to draw the investors' attention.

7.4 BOTTOM UP VS TOP DOWN

In the long list of common mistakes of the entrepreneur presenting his activity, there is one that properly concerns the estimate of own market share.

The market share will then be used to obtain the business potential. What is the sentence that is more often heard?

The entrepreneur starts talking about a huge potential market and then exclaims: "If we're able to penetrate at least 1% of the market, we would have already achieved a remarkable outcome".

The entrepreneur tries to get the message across that on such a huge market, and so very interesting, it will need small effort for his business to be successful. In fact, usually, covering 1% of own potential market corresponds to overestimated sales.

The problem is that this 1% of market share is often an unsubstantiated estimate.

In Reality Check, G. Kawasaki defines this approach with the name of Top Down, and suggests overturning the approach into what he calls Bottom Up.

Let's get a look at an example.

Imagine you run a business that is producing and marketing innovative GPS systems in the United States. Your market clearly belongs to that of sold cars.

Top Down Approach:

In the United States, 150 million cars are sold every year. If you achieve 1% of the market, you could sell 1.5 million GPS systems. The next step would be to promote the quantity sold at an average price in order to get an estimate of the revenues.

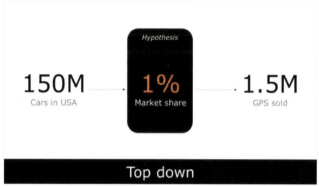

Figure 4 - Estimate market share - Top Down

As you can see, we are trying to say that even with a very small market share, the resounding outcome is achieved. However, this 1% of market share is a completely unsubstantiated estimate and, moreover, it won't necessarily mean that it will symbolize a small outcome.
You must not be deluded that 1% could seem to be a small figure. Since this is a percentage, it can come to symbolize quite large figures as well.

Bottom Up Approach:

Let's try to overturn our reasoning and start our calculation from the number of GPS systems that our factory can produce daily, assuming you are able to saturate its production capacity. Let's imagine the factory able to produce 100 GPS systems per day.

At this point, we should project into the future in order to have at least an annual range. If on one year there are 240 production days, assuming to produce at full capacity, our factory will produce 24,000 GPS systems per year.

24,000 GPS systems, compared to the initial market of 150 million of cars, would symbolize a market share of 0.02%.

This market share is certainly much smaller than the previous 1%, but it is also much more realistic. Notwithstanding the fact that it underpins very aggressive assumptions, that is that the factory would produce in full all the days of a year, and that all the GPS systems produced are sold is, for sure, more credible than a market share generically estimated as small.

Figure 5 - Estimate market share - Bottom Up

In the end, it is all up to credibility. If you want to show the investor that you have credibility, show sound reasoning, and everything will easy from there.

7.5 THE MARKET NICHE CONCEPT AND WHY WE LIKE IT

Often, the reference market is all a matter of zoom. You could be looking at the computer market at a macro level. If you zoom up on the computer, market you will find out that there are personal computer or professional computers markets. Inside them, there are desktop computers, laptops and netbooks.

Inside the laptops, though, there are 12", 13", 15" and even 17" sizes. In turn, inside these categories it would be possible to define the touch screen laptops from all others.

The 13" touch screen laptop market is a niche compared to the total computer market. Generally speaking, while the market size decreases its competitiveness decreases as well. Obviously, a smaller market has a lower potential.

This latter consideration is what makes a niche market very interesting. In fact, the earnings are definitely lower but, if the competition does not live up to expectations, you could become the leader of the market.

Some people say, "It is better to be a large fish in a small pond than a small fish in the ocean". What do you think of that?

Often staring from a small market with less competition will allow you to acquire market share more quickly and get in on the first customers.

Being operative in a market can teach you a lot, and will provide you the necessary experience to consider an expansion into larger markets.

For this reason, identifying a niche from which to start represents an excellent strategy to attack the market, validating a product/service and developing an interesting future growth.

7.6 PERSUASION APPLIED TO MARKET SIZE

7.6.1 Credibility

Integrity in this case, prevails on everything else! Be honest and build up credible estimates if you want to earn your investors' trust. Pay attention, because on this point, making mistakes could be fatal. If your estimates are inaccurate because you have falsified them, or just because you made some mistake in the calculation, and the investor realizes, you will immediately lose credibility on everything else.

Would you invest your money on an entrepreneur that makes mistakes on the calculations to determine the market where he operates? Imagine then, if you would, finding out that the person that is proposing you the project had inflated the figures in order to gain your attention. I think you got my point.

To be clear on the figures, you must know your market, keeping in mind the first principle of Conger, on which a person's credibility is based.

If in your former employment, or maybe even as a consumer, you have known the market where you are operating and the dynamics that drive its development, you will clearly be perceived as less risky than someone that completely ignores the market where he jumped to operate.

One more, time and experience pays off. What is the alternative to experience? Your network of contacts! Maybe you didn't work directly in that market, but your brother could be a top manager of a great market research company and could supply the required information any time you need it.
Alternatively, your best friend is acknowledged as a sector's influencer, so much so as to be able to contribute something to influence that specific sector's trends.

In these cases, you do not have a direct experience, but you have a preferential access to great experts of the market where you want to operate. Therefore, assuming they trust you, it will be easy to think that you could quickly gain the required experience.

7.6.2 Focus on the audience

The market will also be presented in such a way to be able to touch the right spots that gain attention of the audience you have in front of you.
It seems quite natural, since talking about a market is already interesting for the investors, but there are many ways to present an analysis that shows our project's potential.

You will always have to keep in mind that the investors' interest consists in realizing the maximum profit with the minimum risk, so, when you are presenting the market, you should try to prove that your market will optimize the investor's trade-off.

The market size will allow you to prove the high potential profitability of your start-up and, at the same time, decrease the perceived risk.

> *"You should target existing markets that have a high rate of growth or change market. A market with a potential of a billion dollars will allow you to make some mistakes and grant you time to realize real profit margins"*
>
> **Sequoia Capital** [2]

[2] Francisco S. Homem de Mello, Hacking the Startup Investor Pitch: What Sequoia Capital's business plan framework can teach you about building and pitching your company, Ajax Books, 2014

The larger the market, the greater the chances needed to correct the mistakes.

For what concerns the potential high profitability, you should refer to the calculations shown at paragraph 7.3, and remember to be ambitious!

When it comes to perceived risk, you should be able to convince the investor about your ability to bypass the existing entry barriers and to raise others.

This is the reason why presenting your own registered patent or some protection mechanisms of the intellectual property will interest the investors and quickly gain attention.

If your solution is legally protected and only you can exploit it for a certain amount of time, it will be clear that the risk that someone else would enter in that market and copy you is very low.

Usually, these mechanisms hardly apply to digital realities. In fact, it is impossible to protect the code, and, as the biggest part of digital platforms, it can be easily copied and spread if you have valid technical skills.

Just think of CMS like Wordpress that integrate a countless number of ready topics, which allow you to create a website of a particular type with a minimum investment and, in practice, just a few clicks away.

There are templates that allow you to recreate the most famous social networks in a short time. Nobody can prevent you doing that.

A different situation exists for more material ideas, which can be patented. I have recently supported a start-up that invented a framework for bicycles that would make them unusable if stolen.

When they showed me the problem, it wasn't difficult to believe the figures that were showing how many bicycles are stolen every year, but when they showed me their solution, at the beginning, I found it hard to understand its uniqueness.

Then they explained that their solution is protected by a patent, and this made their idea a unique one. It made the benefit they would provide immediately clear, compared to any other competitor or potential newcomer.

In other cases, maybe the solution cannot be patented, but it is based upon a technology that is so hard to use that it will be difficult to locate the required skills to operate it on the market. This too can create a safety barrier at the entrance and the team section, as we will see later, could become the hinge inside the pitch.

In short, the barriers at the entrance reassure the investor about the fact that investing in you, there will always exist a safety margin, able to protect your investment from potential competitors.

7.6.3 Emotionality

The investors represent an audience that is decisively technical from the economic financial metrics analyses. It is therefore logical to present the figures that represent the market. As you have seen, a quantitative approach will allow you to gain credibility and show off the knowledge of the framework in which you operate.

However, it won't be able to excite the investors with the figures. Even if they are specialists, always remember that they are people.

The metrics are logical, rational, cold and certainly necessary, but are not enough if you really want to breach people's minds.

We have already seen the power of emotions at work, but how could be possible to bring emotion in market sizing metrics?

Metrics are an abstract concept, hardly touchable. Moreover, they are often of high level estimates, and thus not that reliable. Endorsing these figures with realism and personality will allow you to get some abstract metrics close to people.

The best way to do that? From the stories of your integration with customers, or even better, from the customers reviews that could confirm they appreciated your product or service.

If you have developed a solution for the visually disabled and, at a certain point of the presentation, you introduce the positive feedback from some visually impaired customers, you are showing how the market is really behaving with regards to your idea, and provide a face to your figures.

This way, the concept will be much warmer and more personal. The figures will no longer be abstract figures, but people that have the same problem. This will create a much more solid and concrete perception of your market in the eyes of the investors.

This way, exploiting emotions—"humanizing" abstract concepts—will allow you to excite your audience when you speak about market size.

7.7 Summarizing

A correct sizing of the market is critical in order to enhance the potential of your business project and interest the investor. You should aspire to get interesting figures and remember that a structured investor's aim is to get a ten-times return on investment in start-ups. Watch out and make your estimates accurate, or you'll lose the audience's trust.

Build your credibility based on your market knowledge and on your personal relationships, which allow you to get special market insights. Make your figures appealing to the audience and let them perceive them as real by using storytelling or positive testimonials chosen from your clients.

CHAPTER 8

BUSINESS MODEL

An investor pitch is a presentation that is used to collect funding for a business activity. The entrepreneur needs funding in order to make his own company live and grow. The investors need to invest in order to make capital gains and sustain their business model.

The investors invest in order to make a profit, and if they will invest in your company. This will mean that they believe their investment could be fruitful, and they will be able, one day, to sell their shares at a higher price than they have evaluated them at when they invested.

In short, the investors will want back what they have given you, plus more besides, at the end of your relationship!

This is the reason why it is critical to show the investors the models that the business will use in order to make a profit, during the pitch presentation.

If the company earns a profit, it could develop, will increase its value and could, one day, pay back its investors.

However, when we are talking about business models, the pitch becomes complicated, and a series of difficulties arise.

According to Dave McClure, founder of 500 start-ups:

"A start-up is a company that is confused about:
1. What its product is
2. Who its customers are
3. How to earn a profit from it"

Can I have more than one business model? Can I present multiple business models, or is it better to focus only on the main one? How can I represent a business model? What is the information an investor expects to find in this section?

8.1 WHAT IS A BUSINESS MODEL

Peter Drucker, also known as "the founder of modern management", believes that a business model is the set of all answers, among others, to the following questions:

- Who is the end customer?
- In what does the end customer acknowledge my value?
- How do we earn from this business?

In this first definition, some critical aspects for any business model have already surfaced: the end consumer, the interaction between the consumer and the company, and the real earning produced by the model.

Let's go on with another example. In Seizing the White Space, Mark W. Johnson proposes a table of potential business models, relating them to real life business cases.[1]

CAN'T THINK OF A NEW BUSINESS MODEL?
Try adapting one of these basic forms.

ANALOGY	HOW IT WORKS	EXAMPLE
Affinity club	Pay royalties to some large organization for the right to sell your product exclusively to their customers.	• MBNA
Brokerage	Bring together buyers and sellers, charging a fee per transaction to one or another party.	• Century 21 • Orbitz
Bundling	Package related goods and services together.	• Fast-food value meals • iPod/iTunes
Cell phone	Charge different rates for discrete levels of a service.	• Sprint • Better Place
Crowdsourcing	Get a large group of people to contribute content for free in exchange for access to other people's content.	• Wikipedia • YouTube
Disintermediation	Sell direct, sidestepping traditional middlemen.	• Dell • WebMD
Fractionalization	Sell partial use of something.	• NetJets • Time-shares
Freemium	Offer basic services for free, charge for premium service.	• LinkedIn
Leasing	Rent, rather than sell, high-margin, high-priced products.	• Cars • MachineryLink
Low-touch	Lower prices by decreasing service.	• Walmart • IKEA
Negative operating cycle	Lower prices by receiving payment before delivering the offering.	• Amazon
Pay as you go	Charge for actual, metered usage.	• Electric companies
Razor/blades	Offer the high-margin razor below cost to increase volume sales of the low-margin razor blades.	• Printers and ink
Reverse razor/blades	Offer the low-margin item below cost to encourage sales of the high-margin companion product.	• Kindle • iPod/iTunes
Reverse auction	Set a ceiling price and have participants bid as the price drops.	• Elance.com
Product to service	Rather than sell a product, sell the service the product performs.	• Zipcar
Standardization	Standardize a previously personalized service to lower costs.	• MinuteClinic
Subscription	Charge a subscription fee to gain access to a service.	• Netflix
User communities	Grant members access to a network, charging both membership fees and advertising.	• Angie's List

SOURCE *SEIZING THE WHITE SPACE* BY MARK JOHNSON   HBR.ORG

Figure 1 – hbr.org

---

[1] Ovans A., What is a business model?, hbr.org

Among these examples we find:

• Offer free basic services and be paid for premium services – Linkedin

• Reduce prices being paid at the moment of purchase, before the product delivery - Amazon

• Sell directly to the end consumer bypassing intermediaries – Dell

Have you noticed that, in all cases, this is the way the business works? In particular, from this table surface the models you can use to generate profits from the various companies mentioned.

However, you must pay attention not to mix up the business model with revenue streams. In fact, quite often the tendency exists to mix these two concepts, but the business model includes, among its components, the revenue stream.

Let me make an example of what I mean by 'revenue stream'[2]:

Figure 2 - Revenue stream concepts compared

Thanks to this intelligent chart, it is possible to discover that Apple produces most of its revenues thanks to the iPhone, while Google and Facebook, for instance, raise the majority of their revenue from advertising. The revenue streams of these companies are quite clear, but up 'til now, nothing has been said about potential customers, strategic partnerships, main activities, etc.

Revenue streams are one part of the essential components of a business model, but they do not have to be conceptually exchanged, because they are different things.

The business model is something a bit more complex that, in accordance with Drucker, explains the assumptions at the base of a company's operation.

[2] Desjardins J., Chart: here's how 5 tech giants make their billions, visualcapitalist.com

8.2 BUSINESS MODEL CANVAS

Alexander Osterwalder, author of Business Model Generation, has collected and integrated the main assumptions of the basics of a business model in a famous template called Business Model Canvas.

If you are dealing with start-up and have attended any boosting route, you would certainly have heard about them. This is a model used to push entrepreneurs to think about the interaction between all the components of their business model.

A. Osterwalder believes that a business model is based on 9 critical components:

- Value proposition
- Customers Segments
- Relationships with customers
- Revenue streams
- Channels
- Key activities
- Key Partners
- Key Resources
- Cost Structure

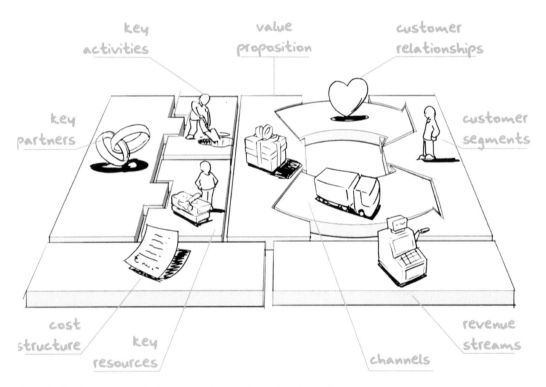

Figure 3 - The 9 components of a business model according to A. Osterwalder

Value proposition

We have already defined the value proposition in the 'Solution' chapter. To add an example to those lessons, and in relation to this, let's use Google's value proposition: "Share the world's knowledge".

Segments of customers

Who are your customers? Are they consumers, people (business to consumer), or businesses (business to business)? Facebook, for instance, is B2C — if you think of it as social networks that people use in order to stay in touch with friends — but it is B2B if you think of the advertising system that they sell to companies.

Relationships with the customers

Every business interacts with its own customers. The way it interacts, however, can vary. For example:

• Customer service—think of the call center of telephone companies.

• Account manager dedicated to the customer—typically for strategic customers.

• Self-service—interaction managed through prearranged tools and interfaces.

• Automatic Interactions—think of marketing automation mechanisms at the basis of the creation of the mailing list.

• Communities—now we just talk about this, even Facebook is focusing all on the development of the communities.

These are some examples of interactions that a business could have with its clients. In many cases, they can coexist within the same business that is segmenting and managing its own customers differently.

Revenue flows

The manner through which a business monetizes its own clients.

Channels

The channels refer to the ways in which a business makes its products/services available to the customers. For example, Apple sells through Apple stores, but also sells online and through partnerships with great electronic distribution center chains (e.g. Mediaworld).

Key activities

The most important activities are directly connected to the company's value proposition. In practice, they consist of the activities that the business uses to create value to its client. Taking an example from my past, developing consultancy services that would improve the processes of the business's own clients – Accenture.

Key Partners

Key partners are the relationships used for the development and creation of a company's activities. A typical example is the relationship with a company's own suppliers.

Key Resources

Key resources are required on a long-term basis for the proper functionality of all corporate activity. The resources can be of financial, human, physical or intellectual nature. In a consultancy company, they could be the employees. In the accounting sector, we talk about CapEx—capital expenditures—the expenditures strictly connected to the company's activity.

Cost structure

When we talk about cost structure, we speak of fixed operating expenditures and variable costs connected to the development of corporate activity. They are not required expenditures alongside the Capex, but are important expenditures for company sustainability.

After describing any item of the outline above, I present the famous canvas that will allow you to relate, in an intelligent manner, to all the elements mentioned above.

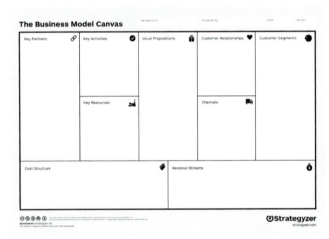

Figure 4 - Business model canvas

The canvas model is an incredible instrument to map the business operating model and make it comparable to the business's competitors.

Moreover, if exploited and investigated in the first stages of the start-up, this can be built into a model that helps the entrepreneur ponder and piece together the plugs of his idea. I realize that, if it is the first time that you look at the canvas, it could seem to be a bit abstract. So let's get together to look at an example of how to use it.

Here is the outcome of the canvas application when you apply it to the launch of the iPod in the early 2000s.

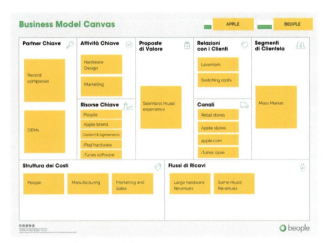

Figure 5 - www.businessmodelcanvas.it

The canvas presents a complete image of the business model of the iPod project. If you look at it with care, you will notice the way the canvas is designed really makes sense. In fact, you will see that the 'pro' value sits in the middle, and splits the internal side of the company (partners, resources, activities and costs) from the external side—that is, the market and the way in which the company achieves it (relationships, channels, customers segments, revenue flows).

The canvas business model is a very complete tool, useful to all entrepreneurs who wish to have a clear picture of their own business. However, it is a mistake to enter the canvas directly into the presentation of the pitch to the investor. The model is too rich with data, and is more a brainstorming tool than a presentation element. Present the business model in a simple and intuitive way.

8.3 SUSTAINABILITY OF THE BUSINESS MODEL

There are two magical metrics widely used in the start-up world which immediately show the sustainability of a business model.

Customer lifetime value (LTV):

The CLV is a prediction of the net profit attributed to future relationships with a client.

"The total gain expressed in net current value that a business predicts to gain from a long term commercial relationship with a client".[3]

In short, it is the value that a client generates towards the company during the lifecycle of their commercial relationship.

Customer Acquisition Cost (CAC)

The CAC represents the expenditures required to acquire a new client. In order to calculate this, you should consider the marketing and sale expenditures in a given period of time, the salaries of the resources committed in this activity, and then divide them for the number of clients acquired in the reference period.

It seems logical that a sustainable business model will show LTV > CAC. However, all too often, the entrepreneurs have a thought clear in their mind of how much a user is yielding (LTV), but overlook the CAC.

E.g., You want to sell an ebook. You write new content, you format it and uploaded the finished product on your new website, ready to be distributed in PDF format to readers all over the world.
In order to interest the readers and to capture their emails, you have decided to distribute a short excerpt of your book for free, in exchange for the compilation of a form which requires nothing more than a first name and an email address. Let's assume, for ease of calculation, that readers will only buy the full ebook after having read the excerpt. The book sells some copies, but the website does not generate sufficient traffic. Let's say that your book has a conversion rate of 6% on the excerpt, then 2% on the purchase.

Imagining to have 2000 visitors per month, your book would sell only 2 copies every month.

- Monthly Traffic   2000
- Excerpt   6%
- Purchase   2%
- Price   € 10.00
- Copies sold   2.4
- Revenues   € 24.00

This seems an interesting model. Everything is automated, you have to do almost nothing and the book is selling all over the world. But you want more!

You decide to increase the traffic and launch a Google Adwords campaign. Every click will cost you €0.10. In order to acquire a client and sell one copy, you will need around 833 clicks (1/(6%*2%)). That means every new client will cost you €83.

It is plain to see that this business model is not sustainable, because a user generates only €10 per copy sold and there is no way to price the ebook higher than €83.

This is where you create selling and cross-selling strategies in order to monetize users acquired in other ways.

If, for example, your book is explaining how to use software that you have developed and are selling online with

---

[3] Customer lifetime value, businessdictionary.com

a subscription model of €100/year. At that point, the book becomes only a tool to acquire clients, as you are actually doing business on the software.

Take into consideration the conversion rate of the readers that become those that purchase the software. One of the most traditional examples is the example of the movie theatre that sells tickets, but in fact realizes the major part of its revenues by selling soft drinks and popcorn.

From the CAC optimization viewpoint, there are many possible alternatives. In fact, Google Adwords is often considered to be a quite costly acquisition method. Much often, people go to Facebook Advertising in order to get an acquisition at lower prices but, in any case, these tools require you to be expert in order to be fully utilised, and so you should also consider the costs of the resource.

In brief, by acting well on the LTV and CAC balance, you will to build up a sustainable business model.

As you can see in the above chart, the recurrent revenue will improve the client's LTV, thanks to the fact that once a client has been acquired once, they will keep on paying a subscription in the long term.

Cross/Up selling can also improve the LTV because they monetize a client that has already been acquired via different methods.

Another interesting observation is the impact of the product's growth viral effects. When a client, through word of mouth, is disseminating the product and allows you to acquire for free new clients the CAC is spread on a wide basis and will result lower on average.

What can drive the balance

Figure 6 - Levers to balance LTV and CAC according to D. Skok

8.4 A PITCH BUSINESS MODEL

Looking at the pitches examined some interesting observations come up.

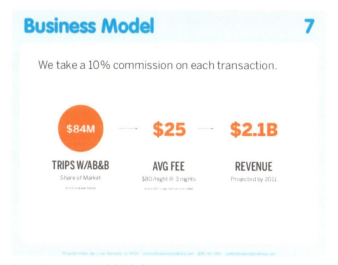

Figure 7 - Business model Airbnb

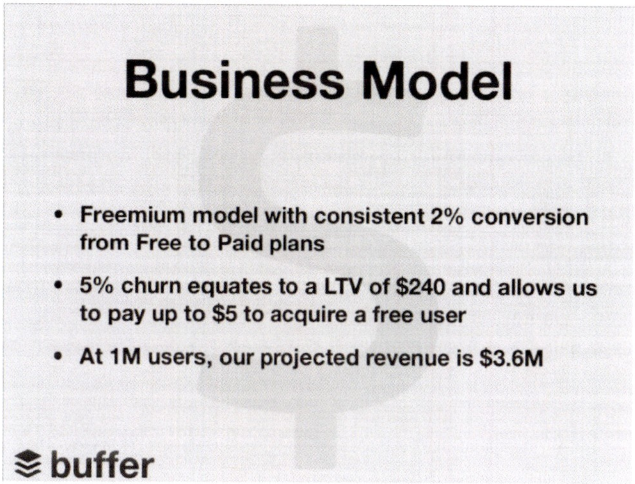

Figure 8 - Business model Buffer

In the case of Airbnb, this business model is mixed in a slide together with some market metrics. The slide goal is to show an estimate of potential revenues projected into 2011. In this slide, the business model would be, *"We are retaining 10% of commission on any transaction"*.

The business model sentence explains the company's model to generate revenue. In addition, it is well summarized and easy to understand. A simple and brief sentence that speaks clearly to the investors is all you need inside a business model slide.

The case of Buffer shares some similarities with Airbnb—in fact, it's easy to notice the sentence related to the business model is at the top: *"Freemium model with a solid 2% of conversion rate between free model and payment model"*.

The second sentence is connected to model sustainability and explains that, based upon the *customer lifetime* value calculated as a function of the churn rate, the company can pay up to $5 for the acquisition of any single user.

To clarify the technicalities behind this sentence, it is important to clarify the concept of churn rate[4]:

The CR is the percentage of subscribers to a service that will delete their subscription within a given period of time. In practice, it is the percentage of your clients that will cease to be your clients.

Let's make an example that could explain both metrics we have mentioned. Imagine that you are selling a software with a subscription. Your website sells 10 subscriptions per month, and so 120 per year. The second year, assuming a zero

[4] Churn rate, investopedia.com

growth rate, you will sell 120 more subscriptions and so at the end of that year you will have 240 subscribers.

It would be nice if any client that purchases a subscription would remain loyal for the rest of his/her life, but in reality, it is not so. Some subscriptions get canceled and it is important that you are taking this into account whenever you are making economic-financial predictions.

Assuming a 10% churn rate per year every year, 12 users will cancel their subscription, therefore you will get to the second year having 240-24 clients "burned" which corresponds to a total of 226 active clients.

In some cases, the churn rate gets a crucial meaning, especially for an investor. Imagine a start-up that acquires many new users every day, but that, after having tested the service, will cease to use it.

In such cases, the start-up could show phenomenal client acquisition figures, but a shrewd investor could ask how many of those users will really keep using the service, and would soon realize that these are just users testing the system and then, for whatever the reason, will discontinue it.

Going on with this example, the churn rate could be an excellent alarm bell. In fact, just looking at the acquisition metrics, you risk being distracted. Conversely, to a more careful analysis, which would consider the churn rate too, you could find out that, despite the interest for your product/service, the clients won't meet their expectations, and so it is better to explore, maybe with some questionnaires, to understand the problems to focus on.

In short, the churn rate is a magical metric that is very important for many business models.

Finally, going back to the Buffer example, the third sentence shows the revenue potential as reflected in the number of users. This is a clear attempt to make a metric that otherwise would be quite unappealing interesting to the investors (how much are 1 million users worth?).

In brief, the three sentences are the components of a business model but, I believe that the operating mechanism would deserve a dedicated slide.

The case of LinkedIn is more in line with my idea of what information to show in a pitch talking about the business model.

LINKEDIN SERIES B DECK

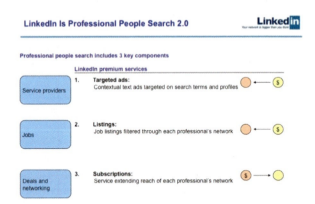

Figure 9 - Linkedin business model

LinkedIn assigns a name to three different business models and describes them briefly. That there is an important room for improvement from a 'content graphic' design standpoint, but the central part is of the illustration is crucial in order to explain the three models of operation of the business.

Finally, going back to the Airbnb model, I personally would have redesigned that slide emphasizing the business model of operation:

Figure 10 - Alternative proposal for business representation of Airbnb model

In this representation, I have no chart purpose, but I feel the investor could understand at first sight how the company intends to make its business work.

8.5 PERSUASION APPLIED TO THE BUSINESS MODEL

8.5.1 Credibility

I remember the project of a start-up that was developing a new social network.

Because of the social network nature, as big names have already shown, the most natural business model is the advertising one.

On one hand, there are users that use the service, often for free, while the platform takes care of collecting their data and profile them. The more rich and accurate the database, the greater the interest from perspective new clients to access, advertise there or with other requests.

For this reason, social networks need to get to the so-called 'critical mass' of users, so that they begin to have a relevant value on the market.

The start-up appears to have quite varied and confusing business models. One of these was definitely the advertising one, similar to Facebook. But amongst the various business models, I remember one that would have turned that social network into an eCommerce site.

The funny thing was that the eCommerce site would have completely distorted the social network's very essence, since they are two completely different things!

However, the entrepreneur believes that many business models raise the investor's interest. Such an approach raises the total inexperience of the entrepreneurial team, which had never developed any social network before and none of the members have never been in the past an entrepreneur, nor had any experience in the digital world.

The presence of many possible business models backfired against the entrepreneurial team, undermining the credibility that even the first one, the more natural one, could ever be implemented.

That team had no experience and did not know anyone that could support them in order to fill up that gap. Experience and know-how are the crucial pillars of your credibility. If you lose credibility in one step, all the rest will be lost.

If you have no experience, you should be well informed on the successful business models in your type of start-up. Alternatively, always remember that purchasing skills on the market or promoting relationships that could satisfy such lack could help you.

Finally, keep in mind the importance of tests that validate hypotheses supporting the business plan. For instance, you could validate the channels to reach the client or price thresholds. We will go over this in a more detailed manner in the chapter dedicated to it.

8.5.2 Focus on the audience

I remember a start-up that was presenting a new eCommerce to some investors. This was an eCommerce of physical products, and so it had to face the great criticality of logistics. In fact, the digital process of any eCommerce of physical products ends when the purchase ends, when the product physically reaches the final customer.

The entrepreneur, after a careful search on the investors' profiles, discovered that one of them had invested a lot on eCommerce sites, and had engaged in partnership relationships with a courier, on a national level in order to offer more beneficial conditions to all the eCommerce start-ups in his portfolio.

Knowing this, at a certain point during his pitch, he did two very smart moves: at first, he pointed out the criticality of having to manage logistics, making reference to the latter as one of the most critical and dangerous points of investing in his activity. This way, he showed an awareness of the risks related to his business model and showed sensitivity towards the investor and his risk. This made him gain trust, just working on a his own point of weakness.

Secondly, he directly called upon the assistance of the investor, declaring his interest to be part of the investor's portfolio, since he could make available to him interesting interplays.

This small anecdote shows how presenting a business model that could be considered traditional and well-rooted on the market, could suddenly become interesting if narrated in away that addresses the interests of the people in front of you.

8.5.3 Emotionality

As we have already seen about market sizing, metrics charts are cold and will not generate any emotion in your audience. The chart is important, especially for an audience of investors that has gained experience in many business models and those which could represent the criticalities that risk to lead to failure the start-up.

By showing a clear and complete chart, you will be able to show the investor that you already took into consideration the key variables, and that you are aware of the elements to keep an eye on.

However, up 'til now, you have reinforced your credibility, but you have not excited anyone. The way to excite consists of taking advantage of anecdotes or stories.

Narrate the story of one client that has purchased your product. Tell them of how he interacted with your sales channels, if he interacted with the website, it would be nice to show a video of the session recorded by the customer when purchasing.

You do not have to limit this to intangible evidence though. Give a name to this person, give him/her a face and, if you can, get an interview in order to find out what he/she thinks of his/her purchase.

Bring to life the people who your business model operates amongst, and you will see everything will look more interesting and emotionally captivating for your audience.

8.6 Summarizing

The business model sums up the operation of your activity. Osterwalder's canvas will allow you to convey the most important nine founding elements, and to relate them amongst themselves.

Generally, we do not present the whole canvas in a pitch, but we will focus on the planned layout of the main components.

Pay attention to the consistency of your business model with the type of start-up you are presenting. It doesn't take much to let the experienced investor understand if you really are experienced, if you have at least studied, or if you know absolutely nothing.

Do not mix too many business models in your pitch presentation, show just one—the main one—and mention the other models as potential developments. Expose yourself to possible risks or doubts as little as you can, and show solid foundations for at least on one model.

CHAPTER 9

TRACTION

Any start-up is born from an idea. How many times have you found yourself talking with your friends on a future project to conquer the world? How many times, during a "pizza and beer" night with your fellow students have you thought about the new app or a new revolutionary website that could change the situation in the market?

The ideas can be great, for sure. The problem is that they will often remain only thoughts shared between friends.

You cannot think of showing to an investor an idea that exists only on your slides, and which that never "hit the ground". Remember that the investor wants to get the highest performance with the minimum risk. If you are showing something that exists only in your head, the risk perceived will be higher.

Traction is the magical word that make the hairs prickle to any investor, but often is one of the things that we are not able to show in our pitches. Why is it so hard to collect and show the first traction metrics?

What is the key information that should be presented in our pitch in order to show good traction and interest to the investors? What should you do in order to appear credible while showing results? Just how much should you go into, in order to have reasonably interesting metrics?

9.1 METRICS AND COMMON MISTAKES

I think that any entrepreneur, in his life, has to take one of the most over-used answers from an investor: *"Not a bad idea, come back when you have more traction"*.

> *"Traction is, for sure, one of the most used words by VC. But it is also an abbreviation that people use to talk about the grip of a project on the market. Many investors could ask you for the business model. We believe instead that the traction is the most difficult part to show"* [1]
>
> **Fred Wilson, Principal, Union Square Ventures**

Why do investors seem look for nothing but that? Traction shows that the customers really want your product, and so it confers credibility and safety to the investment.

How do you measure traction? According to the start-up type, you cannot think for sure that everything can be reduced to only one KP[2]. Moreover, it would not necessarily be that traction should measure itself with economic-financial metrics.

Brenda Baker, VC Greylock, proposes key metrics according to the sector where the start-up operates (see the following figure).[3]

eCommerce	Fashion Q&A Consumer Internet product	Premium SaaS product for small business
Revenue growth	User numbers	Revenues
Average sales or gross margins	Engaged users and type of engagement	Conversion to paid customers
Customers	Virality	Registered users
Average return visits/customer	Partnerships	Customer acquisition costs
Units sold		Lifetime value/customer
		Distribution partners
Enterprise	**Retail**	**Consumer Products**
Revenues	Revenue growth	Units sold
Number of clients	Units sold	Revenues
Average contract size	Average sales or gross margins	Number of retail outlets product sold in
Qualified sales pipeline	Customers	Distribution partners
	Lifetime value/customer	

Figure 1 - Examples of metrics to measure traction

This table can help you understand how a few key parameters would suffice to define the correct performance in a given sector. I invite you not to take them as an absolute reference, because I believe that it would be specific, and thus need a dashboard of parameters designed ad hoc.

Traction is a tangible and unquestionable evidence of the fact that customers want your product.

In Alfred's pitch at Techcrunch Disrupt, already mentioned many times, there is a moment when Marcela commences: *"[…]We know that Alfred works. All these pins represent the active Alfreds in Boston, and the red ones have been with us for more than 10 months, with a retention rate of 90%[…]"*.

Figure 2 - Marcela Sapone shows a traction for Alfred

As you see, Marcela has not shown a single figure, but with this chart, she has clearly shown that her service was adopted by the market and that customers are paying in order to access it.

---

[1] usv.com
[2] I KPI (Key Performance Indicator) rappresentano misurazioni quantificabili del miglioramento o del peggioramento delle prestazioni in un'attività fondamentale per il successo dell'azienda, ibm.com
[3] How to get startup traction & social proof, fundable.com

If, for instance, you have a product on pre-sale, and the customers are paying a small amount in advance in order to be awarded the product you have just launched, then you can say to have the first signs of traction. As you see, the product does not exist yet and at the moment, maybe you are only working with a pre-sale page that has nothing to do with the whole process of selling that you will implement later on.

However, this could be enough to convince an investor that people want that product and that they would agree to accept your price.

Popular again is the concept of a 'minimum viable product', essential to collect the first traction metrics.

My advice then when you are collecting the traction metrics is to use metrics that are real and significant. This is not only good for the pitch presentation, but mostly for yourself, so that you have a close measurement of the progress of your project.

When you are launching your new website, you will typically collect the first 200/300 registered users that try it in few days. Much too often, I see start-ups publicising the first hundred or so users as if they were the tangible evidence that the market is going crazy for your idea.

For the most part, the first hundred or so contacts are relatives and friends of the start-up founding members.

Do not convince yourself, and don't try to convince the investors with these figures, because misleading yourself will only cause blunders, and because those investors with a minimum of experience are perfectly aware of such dynamics.

My next piece of advice is connected to the famous questionnaires, submitted with some hundreds of answers from customers that are confirming their interest in the project. Usually, the questionnaires the entrepreneurs submit to their customers require no commitment as a consequence of the answers. As a result, he interviewed people often will answer positively in order not to disappoint the entrepreneur absorbed in his dreams of glory.[4]

When you are measuring and showing your traction, try to be as concrete and credible as possible. If you have many friends that, in order to show you their support, would register to the website, skim them and evaluate the users that are really interested in the product.

Another example, again from a winner of the Techrunch Disrupt, is Agrylist, already examined beforehand, up to the solution part. After having showed the demo, as in the case of Alfred, the founder says, *"We know there is a need for Agrylist and we know that it works. We released the beta version two months ago, and we already have got 6 greenhouses using it, allowing us to produce income".*

In doing this, the entrepreneur is showing that there are already active customers using the product.

Figure 3 - Agrylist showing traction

---

[4] To know more about client interview technique, i advise you the book The Mom Test by R. Fitzpatrick, 2013

Among the pitches examined before, LinkedIn's presentation for round B shows a slide with the promised outcome in round A, and would compare it with the outcome really achieved[5]. In short, the chart shows that the outcome achieved is significantly greater than what has been promised, conquering the investors' trust.

In fact, the investors could naturally think, "If they have already succeeded in being better than what they promised, why couldn't they do that again?"

You can show traction also by examining the metrics you have been able to achieve during your journey. The investors are inclined to think that if you achieve good outcome in the past, you are able to get the outcome you would like to achieve in the future.

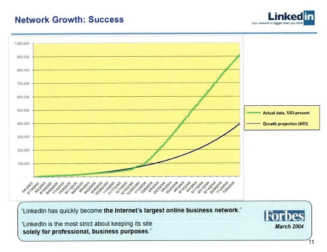

Figure 4 - LinkedIn's traction

---

[5] Hoffman R., LinkedIn's Series B Pitch to Graylock, reidhoffman.org

9.3 Summarizing

All entrepreneurs should be aware of the importance of calculating and presenting traction metrics. The metrics allow entrepreneurs to earn the investors' trust and to more consciously manage the project.

The start-up won't often have solid traction metrics, and various scenarios can open up where patents or tests supplement the lack of solid evidence on the market.

The best scenario would be the one where you are able to show that your project will generate, paying customers in a sustainable manner (LTV > CAC), who continue to use the service and spread their voice to their acquaintances.

Traction is a crucial section that supports and shows the importance of the problem, the strength of the solution, and the validity of the business model for market sizing estimates.

CHAPTER 10

COMPETITION

You have worked well so far, having identified a significant problem, building a solid solution, and you have been able to present a business model that allowed you to create a sustainable activity to investors.

At this point I am asking you, *"Are you sure to be the only one answering your problem?"*. Wait a moment before answering me instinctively, and make sure you are certain of your answer. Who could do the same in your town, village, in the world… Now, I ask you again, are you really sure?

In this chapter, you will find that neither of the answers you gave are important. When you are talking about competition, the investors' attention will immediately focus on some key points.

Who are your competitors? What if you have none? What if they are quite strong? What is the importance, if the competitors only operate abroad?

Let's look at the matter in detail in this interesting section of the pitch!

10.1 UNIQUE, INDEED, BUT IN THE WAY OF DOING IT!

Let's go back to the question I asked in the chapter's preface: are you really sure you are the only one able to solve this problem on the market? This is a common question that investors ask entrepreneurs.

For the most part, entrepreneurs will answer with certainty, yes, they assert to be the only ones to have detected a problem and to try to solve it.

Thus, begins the typical scene. The investor with his iPad in hand, accesses Google, and looks for similar solutions to the one presented by the investor. He quickly identifies some, and starts asking more questions.

Here the entrepreneur, embarrassed, is taken by surprise because he does not know all of the competitors mentioned. However, the investor, if you think deeply, has had no time to make a super detailed search. He probably read out only the results on the first page.

The entrepreneur has been caught red handed while lying, has been shown to be unprepared. This is the winning mix to immediately lose the audience's trust. On this point, I agree with the investor. It is inconceivable that an entrepreneur would not be prepared on such an important factor as his competition.

For the most part, even the most brilliant ideas have competitors on the market. This is not a problem at all; instead, it is a wonderful sign for the investors. Do you know why? Because if the market is populated, that means that there is a market for your idea.

If you were the only one on the market, investors may think that the market does not exist. Of course, it could be that you invented a new market, but that would be a very risky investment, compared to investing in another start-up operating in an existing and tested market (even if by other competitors).

Having competitors is a healthy thing for a company; it means that you are heading the right way. Being the only product or service on the market is not the point, but being the only one able to solve the problem in a certain way is what you need to look for. You shall be the one to introduce an original solution much better than the existing ones. This is the reason why you should always show your ranking compared to competitors.

In the introduction and launch of the first iPhone in 2007, Steve Jobs said, *"Telephones on the market today are not smart, and are absolutely not easy to use. The smartphones are a bit too smart, but are not easy to use because of their plastic keyboard. We have invented a smart telephone, extremely easy to use"*.[1]

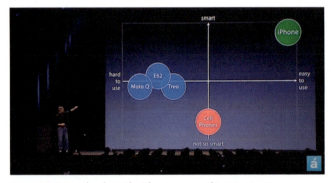

Figure 1 - Steve Jobs places the iPhone compared to its competitors

The way he introduced the iPhone is direct, and very effective too. Without figures and complex charts, Steve Jobs identified the strongest diversification points of his new product, and placed it in relation to all the others.

[1] Steve Jobs – iPhone Introduction in 2007 (Complete), youtube.com

In the case of telephones, everyone knew the competitors at the time, and everyone knew the existence of mobile phones, so this matrix was easy to understand. However, the most interesting thing is that it makes it plain how the market is structured, and why this product is unique compared to the others.

As you can see, Jobs was not scared to show a very populated market. He did not invent the phone, he reinvented it!

What really makes the difference is start-up the execution.

> *"When the entrepreneurs come to me with their million dollar-idea, I must tell them a lot that an idea alone is worth nothing. The game is played on the execution, and the investors invest in people they believe could really realize the ideas or, better yet, in those that have, in their past, some successful executions. The execution makes things happen, and for the start-up, this often means they have to make the change happen, something that is even harder to do"*
>
> **Martin Zwilling,**
> **CEO & Founder of Start-up Professionals**[2]

During my coaching speeches, people always ask, *"What do you think to be harder between the product's development and its marketing?"*. Often, the class is unsure, and didn't know what to choose. Usually, by show of hands, both alternatives are voted in a similar way.

Obviously, the right answer is, *"It depends on chance"*, But the reason why I ask this question is that often you take it for granted that, once the product is made available, people will buy it.

One often hears, *"As soon as we go online, the website will take off by itself"*. Certainly, there are cases so brilliant that have been able to attract such viral interest in the market soon after their launch, but these are famous cases that are quite rare.

Citando Systrom, Founder of Instagram, says:

"[…] in few minutes, the downloads started happening from all the parts of the world. We passed 10,000 users in one hour, and I thought it would really be the best day of my life. At the end of the day, the growth was unstoppable, so much so that I asked myself if we had been properly counting.

The much-yearned night of sleep, after so much work, transformed in a few hours into a run to the office in order to add capacity to the service.

At the end of the first week, Instagram had been downloaded 100,000 times. Another week, and it reached some more 100,000 users that downloaded the app. Within two months, Instagram reached the first million users […]".[3]

---

[2] Zwilling M., Startups are all about the execution, so tell me how, forbes.com

[3] Markowitz E., How Instagram grew from Foursquare knock-off to $1 Billion photo empire, inc.com

Instagram went live at 12.15 am on 6 October, and around the middle of December, some months after, it reached one million users. Keep these figures in mind when you are writing your roadmap. Be ambitious, but always try to keep your feet on the ground. The moment you decide to assert reaching one million users in a few months, consider that you are saying you will replicate Instagram's success!

The execution is what makes the difference. Let's think about that. When Facebook was launched in 2004, the market was already controlled by other similar social media sites, among which is the most famous one, MySpace.

Figure 2 - When Facebook was launched it was not alone

In a very short time, a small group of teenage college students made possible the impossible.
How did that happen?

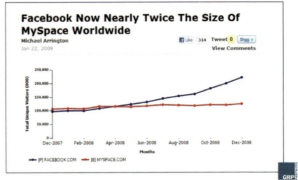

Figure 3 - Facebook vs MySpace [4]

I am not a technical person, but I don't believe that Mark had in his PC such an advanced technology that MySpace, in their office, didn't have available.

If you search online, you will find various articles by many influencers, entrepreneurs, investors and experts of the sector that will provide their opinion. One of the most acclaimed thesis is the one on design and of the difference in usability. MySpace allowed all the users to fully customize their own page, and so surfing the users' profiles felt like browsing a real circus. Most of the profiles were impossible to surf, and obviously the website reflected that.

Facebook instead created minimalist graphics, leaving no chance to customize profiles. This way, all the users had the same profile of anyone else, if not for the contents, and homogeneity made surfing and browsing easier and more pleasant everyone.

[4] Suster M., Social networking: the present, techcrunch.com e Arrington M., Facebook now nearly twice the size of MySpace worldwide, techcrunch.com

Another acclaimed thesis connects Facebook exclusivity in the launching stage. While MySpace was available for everyone, Facebook was only available for students of some colleges, and therefore was a privilege for few people. This made it desirable by everyone, and such desire seemed to have triggered its expansion.

There are other people that believe that Facebook had been farsighted in creating groups of people and exploiting the communities. In fact, according to this theory, the strength of the social networks does not consist of the ability to make everyone connect with others, but to connect people that are significant between each other. In the case of Facebook, it is being connected to our own friends. Nowadays, this is more true to the evolution of the groups and Facebook's focus on communities.

Someone else asserts that Facebook's strength had been not to flood users with advertising, especially in the initial stages when that social media platform took off. In the same years, MySpace was a showcase of advertising banners.

Independently from either of these, and the many other theories that can be found, would be the most acclaimed one. What they have in common is that they are all different ways to bring an idea to life. There are various different ways to create an execution.

For this reason, I believe that you shouldn't be afraid to acknowledge the value our competitors have, and to place them correctly on the market. However, you should be aware of the outstanding features of your company, and how to exploit them in order to surface on the market.

10.2 PORTER'S 5 STRENGTHS MODEL

With the word 'competition', we usually refer to other players on the market that make—or could make—your job, and so 'steal you customers' and subtract market shares from you.

In fact, according to Michael Porter, competition in one sector is influenced only in part by direct competitors. According to Porter, there exist 5, now famous, strengths that control competition that a company will face on the market, and direct competitors are only one of them.[5]

I am proposing a summary of the model, because I believe that it would be extremely useful in order to define your strategic place, and to identify the strengths that could generate opportunities or threats for your business.

What follows represents an exemplification of the model for teaching purposes. If you find it interesting, I invite you to deepen that on dedicated books and articles.

Figure 4 - Porter's five strengths model

[5] Porter M.E., How competitive forces shape strategy, hbr.org

POTENTIAL NEW ENTRANTS

New entrants are companies that bring innovation or companies that, being already strong in other sectors, adopt strategies to differentiate and attack new markets.

In any case, if the entry strategy works, they will conquer a share of the market, diminishing the profit among the sector's current players.

The defense strategy towards these new entrants consists of promptly raising some barriers at the entry. So the threat of the entry of potential new entrants will exclusively depend on the barriers' strength.

Which example of barriers at the entrance could protect those who already have a consolidated position on the market?

1. Economies of scale:

What is the cost advantage stemming from an increase of the output?[6] The economies of scale are created due to the inverse relationship between the amounts produced and cost per unit of the product.

So the greater the number of units produced, the smaller the cost per unit (because the base on which the unit cost is calculated is larger). If, inside the market, there is a company that has operated for many years and is covering a wide slice of customers, there will be many product batches, and so the single product will cost much less than those that, having just come into the market, would produce few products to conquer the first market share. It follows that, in the case of competition based on prices, the new entrant would soon be in difficulty.

[6] Economies of scale, investopedia.com

2. Differentiation of the product:

The brand that makes your product unique. If I invent a competitor drink to Coca Cola, as good as it could be, it will be difficult to compete. The strength of a brand can take on an unsurpassed value in some cases, so much so that it will constitute a solid barrier at the entrance.

3. Intensity of the capital:

There are some sectors where large capitals are needed in order to operate there. In some cases, you need to have important production structures, huge investments in advertising, or you should have the resources to support an entry strategy that would entail negative results. In such cases, the need to have financial resources could constitute an entry barrier.

4. Cost disadvantages:

Think of the proprietary technologies or to the patents, or think of the learning economies needed to fit into a specific market. If a company did exercise lots of time for an activity, it learns how to make it more efficient, and so it could bring some important cost advantages compared to a new entrant. The intellectual property instead constitutes a solid entry barrier, for the simple fact that will ensure an exclusivity on the market.

5. Access to distribution channels:

Let's take into consideration the world of large retail distribution. If you were a new producer of chocolates and you would like to compete against Ferrero, Nestlé, Mars, etc., it would be critical to achieve a competitive distribution, and thus be present as much as possible on mall shelves. Do you understand the power of monitoring the distribution channels?

6. Government policies:

Some sectors are governed by the government that limits the access. For instance, the world of maritime connections is often governed by regional tenders that have the duration of many years. So if you win that tender, you will be able to place your ships and transport passengers; otherwise, you will have to wait for the next tender.

SUPPLIERS

The suppliers can reduce the profit of the companies that operate downstream of their supply chain. For example, in the world of information systems for large companies. SAP and Oracle monopolise the market worldwide.

If your large multinational company is SAP implemented, this means that it is structuring its organisational processes in order to work well with the information system modules. Exchanging SAP with another supplier could have a deep impact on the organisation, such that the cost of change (switching cost) could not be sustainable or make this operation inconvenient. Thus, the SAP supplier will acquire power towards his own clients.

If SAP would decide to increase the supply prices to its clients, it could be convenient to pay the surplus instead of changing suppliers. In this case, the clients would be compelled to reduce their margin as a consequence of a weakening relationship towards a strategic supplier.

Another factor that impacts on the suppliers' strength is concentration. If, in the whole market, there is only one supplier from who you can get a certain material, that supplier will acquire power with regards to yourself, and if he decides to increase the prices, you could only comply, reducing your margin or passing the increase downstream to the clients (therefore losing competitiveness).

REPLACEMENT PRODUCTS

An example that I remember from the times I attended a strategy course at the college makes a good point: movies versus theatre.

Theaters are not direct competitors of cinemas, but it can easily subtract customers, proposing an alternative for a night of entertainment.

Trains are airplanes and, on some lines, could absolutely represent replacement products. Think, for instance, the Milano-Roma line.

Another example are maple syrups and sugar. Different types of sugar are amongst their competitors; however, maple syrup proposes to sweeten with a low glycaemic index, representing an alternative, for sure!

Replacement products, although they do not compete between them, can really become competitors. It will be critical to take them into consideration in our own strategy.

INTERNAL COMPETITION

Finally, those that are usually considered direct competitors. These are the guys you should literally know everything about, their lives and achievements! You should know how they are placed on the market, what their prices and technologies are, their competitive factors, their communication strategies and, ideally, their cost structures.

Like we said, having competitors shows that there is a market, and the fact that we are selling means that there are customers willing to pay for a determined product or service. Therefore, you shall study your competitors and define a distinctive, clear position that would seem to be unique to the eyes of the investors.

CLIENTS

Have you ever thought that clients can be another competitive factor? Imagine having a client that is saturates 90% of your production capacity, and the remaining 10% is covered by many small clients. If your main client asks you to lower your prices, he will certainly get your attention.

Obviously, the power of the client relies on how much your product is differentiated and unique. If you are selling milk or petrol, for instance, it would be quite easy to replace you with one of your competitors. But if you are selling iPhones, any other Samsung will not be the same!

The balance amongst the 5 strengths determines the distribution of profit inside an industry. As you can see, the competitors could steal market shares, but it may as well be the suppliers' intervention or the customers' strength that has a direct impact on the profit of those that operate in that sector.

The company's strategy defines the required actions to protect against these strengths trying to counteract an imbalance of the sector.

The 5 strengths model is an important pillar of the modern company's strategy, and I believe that any entrepreneur should at least know its basics.

The five strengths model, similar to the canvas business model in the framework of this book, represents an instrument on which to meditate. I strongly discourage you from directly entering it into your pitch presentation.

There are some considerations on the strategy that may look interesting in the framework of a pitch presentation. For instance, if you are presenting a technology you have patented and that patent constitutes a strong entry barrier for potential new entrants, this could arouse interest of the investors that would normally feel, as we have seen, that such investment a bit less risky.

So, to conclude, you should exploit this model in order to meditate and determine your company strategy, but do not enter it in your presentation with a brutal copy and paste.

10.3 WHAT DOES COMPETITION LOOK LIKE?

In the examined pitches, the competition analysis model recurs more often, for example, if the positioning matrix uses the iPhone presentation by Steve Jobs (see paragraph above) as a base for his own.

Airbnb positions itself as a low-price solution that offers the booking service, while also directly managing the transaction on its platform.

Craigslist, for instance, allows you to locate low-cost overnight stay solutions, but does not allow you to manage the whole acquisition process on the platform.

Figure 5 - Competition matrix from Aribnb pitch

Such a matrix allows you to show the other actors on the market, but this would not necessarily mean that an investor would know your market. Moreover, if during your presentation, he looks for new competitors with his iPad, he would already find them mapped on the matrix.

FrontApp, a collaborative business inbox, financed for 13.25 million dollars, proposes a similar analysis of competitors.

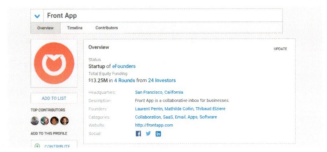

Figure 6 - Frontapp on crunchbase.com

FrontApp differentiates for a better user experience and for a clear targeting of its customers. FrontApp has clearly been designed for business, while many of its other competitors have been developed to please everyone.

Figure 7 - FrontApp Competition matrix

A model I often see when I am supporting start-ups in realizing their pitch is the following infograph:

Figure 8 - Table of comparison with competitors

First of all, this model rarely appears in the pitch analyses on the basis of this book. As you can see, this model is decidedly less intuitive, and longer to be used compared to a positioning matrix.

Remember that a good slide works better if it doesn't steal the attention of the audience from the speaker. The slides support the speaker, not replace him. This table requires more time than the matrix to be processed, and therefore we just do not like it.

Moreover, I think that it would be far clearer to focus on two differentiating factors, feeling secure about their product compared to other people, without entering an endless list of features that are often too detailed.

In short, my advice is to work on few distinct factors, and to present your positioning on a matrix, easy to understand by an investor.

If you judge the merit of all the particular features that differentiate your product from the competitors, there will be a simple way to deepen that during the stages that follow the pitch presentation.

10.4 PERSUASION APPLIED TO COMPETITION

10.4.1 Credibility

When you are presenting your competitors, knowledge and awareness of your competitors are the founding base of your credibility in the eyes of the investors.

At all times, you should avoid being found unprepared when it comes to a competitor the investor knows or that he may have found on the spot.

I remember one occasion when myself and my partner were presenting a start-up of ours to an investor that had been operating on the market for a long time. We were well prepared for the competitors, and had created a nice positioning matrix that would differentiate us, however, showing an interesting market.

The day of the diligence, one partner in the background mentioned a competitor of whom we never have heard of. In that precise moment, ourselves and his team analysts looked for him on the Internet, with no result.

After some minutes of search, we found an old article that referred to the termination of the activity the partner was referring to, and which had happened many years before.

In that moment, I began to breathe easily, but that was the moment when the interrogation burst out. We had to explain the reasons that lead to the failure of the other project which, like our own had been tried in a similar way.

We had to postpone the due diligence session in order to come back with a detailed and complete analysis of that competitor, who was now out of the market.

I am telling this anecdote, about one mistake of mine, because, at times, even the story of those that have preceded us though often hard to locate, have something to teach us.

Try to know your competitors well, find out as many details as possible, and complete the matrix in an exhaustive manner. Always be ready to answer possible questions from the investor.

10.4.2 Focus on the audience

How do you decrease the risk perceived by an investor when you are talking about competition? Simple, especially when you are talking about innovative start-up.

I have recently followed a batch of innovative start-ups in the biomedical world that were proposing hardware and software solutions, which were really interesting.

The beauty of these innovations was that, for the most part, they can be patented, and so I found a slide that recalled the patent to protect the idea of the many start-ups I followed.

Often working in the digital area, I hardly have to look at patents, but in this case, it was on the agenda.

The protection of intellectual property is one of the entry barriers that are defined in Porter's five strengths model. Usually, they are well-liked by the investors, because it reduces the risk that someone else may get through, and be better and quicker than you at the execution.

This one, like all the other factors that differentiate yourself from your competitors in a solid and sustainable way, are elements of great interest for an audience of investors who are trying to assess the risk of investing in your activity.

10.4.3 Emotionality

Imagine telling the story of a competitor that is failing with one of his clients. Studying the story well, you could make sure that the failure would become one point of differentiation with regards to the competitor, and then you would gain the investor attention.

This way, you could easily demonstrate the need of the market to have your solution, and also the difference between your solution and that of a competitor.

Recently on a long duration flight, I watched a film called *The Founder*, inspired by the story of the McDonald chain. If you have not seen it, my advice for you is to watch it. In my opinion, there are interesting entrepreneurial hints in it.

If I had to do McDonald's pitch, I could begin by saying, *"Yesterday, I was at lunch in a drive-in. I waited for more than half an hour for them to bring me a steak, and they finally brought me something else. The female waiters, too concerned not to be picked up, didn't even give me the chance to complain and so, after a long wait, I had to eat something different than what I ordered."*.

As you have seen, I made critical a client's experience that was using a competitor. I hadn't been specific about my competitor's place because, in this case, I am referring directly to the drive-in category. This way, you are knocking out a whole category of competitors.

10.5 Summarizing

With competition, we refer to all the actors of the market that can subtract segments of customers.

Having competitors, for an entrepreneurial activity, is a healthy thing. Don't be scared to show your market, and the people that are operating there.

What will be crucial is to show the positioning that will make unique your product or service compared to your competitors'. The positioning matrix we have seen in this chapter is an excellent tool to use inside the pitch presentation, in order to illustrate your competitors.

CHAPTER 11

GO-TO-MARKET

In the chapter on competition, we have introduced the concept of execution and discussed its importance. A correct execution strategy is the basis of any start-up success. However, an incorrect execution is one of the most common causes of failure.

Execution means to make things happen, and so for an entrepreneur, it means being able to bring his product/service to the market – Go-to-market.

When Ray Kroc asked, the McDonald brothers to being allowed to develop their innovative catering service network for the first time, the brothers answered they had already tried that. However, they abandoned the idea to expand because the association initiatives managed by others had gone out of the owners control.

In fact, McDonald's strength was based upon a few crucial factors at those times:

1. The quality of their products
2. Extreme speed of their service
3. Targeting the menu that included hamburgers, French fries, a drink, and possibly a milkshake

The brothers did notice that many of these pillars, if not all, collapsed when the restaurant was managed by third parties. They even hired someone to perform quality control, but that wasn't enough.

So, surrendering to the idea that nobody else but themselves could carry out the execution of their brand development strategy, they abandoned the idea to expand.

It may seem absurd that such an innovative restaurant was doing so well in one place, couldn't replicate that successful experience in a second, new location.

The problem was that those delegated the activity hadn't been able to take care of the execution in the correct manner.

11.1 MAKE THINGS HAPPEN

There cannot exist only one Go-to-market for all businesses, or according to the company's type. Any case requires a specific strategy connected to the business peculiarity, to the people that are in the team and even to the framework, often dynamic, where we are operating.

Usually, the success of a market approach strategy is born out of many attempts and as many failures.

To the question, *"How did you develop Alfred's customer base in the first months of activity?"* Marcela Sapone answered, *"In the first months, we increased the customer base using dozens of contrivances – traditional postcards under the doors of potential customers, improvised speeches with people at Starbucks, reaching people through Craigslist and Facebook. We did all that could teach us something on peoples' needs, and on the factors that brought them to make their first purchase of a service to ask for help. In the long run, the product itself represents the best marketing tool. The execution is the best sales channel"*.[1]

When Marcela is saying that the product represents the best marketing tool, she is clearly referring to the 'word of mouth' concept. I personally believe that word of mouth is something magical and that, when experimented with, it can be a great privilege for any entrepreneur.

However, word of mouth is the consequence of a successful Go-to-market; the product has arrived in the customers' hands and they liked it so much that they have turned into ambassadors. Your customers have suggested that product to their acquaintances, and convinced them to purchase it.

As you can see, for all of this to happen, you need to have acquired the first clients.

Have you ever seen a successful start-up and asked yourself what were the magical ingredients that the founder combined to get so successful? The practical reality, besides fabulous beaches and myths to recycle onto successful entrepreneurs, is that they are extremely determined to never to give up.

Acting in a proactive way and with the right openness, they accept their mistakes and work in order to avoid to repeat making them. Learning requires great determination.

This is the way to do business, developing and demonstrating the best Go-to-market strategy for your own product.

Entrepreneurs always have an idea about how to reach their customers and bring their product onto the market. However, as far as they can tell, no idea is the right one until some tests will confirm that it works.

As an entrepreneur, you will always have the instinct that will make you think one route is better than the other ones, and it is the proper way. You will never run out of ideas on this route. But you must pay attention, not to be betrayed by your own instinct. Try it, quantify it and decide. Always go this way, and you gain many surprises!

Your customers will astound you much more often than you think, so my advice is to be ready to approach the market with a dynamic mind, open to changes and with a great desire to learn from your mistakes.

---

[1] How do you get early traction for your startup, blog.producthunt.com

11.2 LET'S INTRODUCE GO-TO-MARKET

In the Go-to-market section, we shall so explain how we intend to bring our product/service to the market.

Looking at the pitches above, the best example is Airbnb. We've used their pitch a lot because I believe it is really well structured. In this case, it also presents the information I want to show you.

Figure 1 - Airbnb Go-to-market

In the Go-to-market section, what they call adoption strategy presents three market approach strategies: the first one is connecting to accommodate tourists on the occasion of great events, the second one exploits strategic partnerships, and the third strategy is the Go-to-market technique that has become famous as one of the most brilliant growth hacks in the history of digital start-up.

At the beginning, Airbnb had to overcome the problem of balance between supply and demand. Concerning the supply, usually this is simple because entering apartments in the system is just a matter of a few clicks. The real challenge is to bring these apartments to the attention of travellers that were looking for an alternative to hotels.

At the time, in the absence of Aribnb, a portal people used to search for accommodation was a Craigslist portal, where homeowners posted an advertisement related to their apartment, and people looking for an accommodation for the duration of their trip could contact them.

Craigslist was not managing any transactions happening outside the platform, but it had a huge user database to advertise to.

So the Airbnb team developed an algorithm that allowed the homeowner posting his apartment on Airbnb to share his post automatically on Craigslist. That post on Craigslist then had a link that interested users could use to land on Airbnb, where they could then manage the transaction.

In practice, they were stealing traffic from Craigslist in order to pass it to Airbnb. This operation has allowed Airbnb an explosive growth, and when Craigslist stepped in to block this mechanism, it was too late.

Besides the fact that this story is extremely fascinating from my viewpoint, and I am inviting you to look into it further online[2], the reason I tell you that is to show you that you will rarely find a standard Go-to-market that someone else has realized, and that you can simply replicate for success.

There are too many variables involved that influence any company to make a sure and general plan. The context of the business, the time it operates, its team, the market, etc.

---

[2] AIRBNB: the growth story unveiled, medium.com

The only way to find your own route is by testing and measuring the results. Depending on what is happening, you will learn and react, often in a very creative way.

Airbnb presents, concisely, the key elements of its market access strategy, which will solve the main challenges of their business model: the acquisition of apartments and advertising visibility.

The second case I want to show you is Buffer.

Figure 2 - Buffer Go-to-market

Buffer is an instrument that allows you to plan the sharing of your contents to the main social media networks. What could be an intelligent way to bring into sight of their potential consumers?

The users of buffer are the readers of the web: anyone reads a blog post, an article or any digital content and wants to share it.

Buffer had 6 integrations, and is currently developing the integration with Feedly and Pocket. Feedly is an app that allows you to group all your favorite blogs and comfortably enjoy their contents. Pocket is an app that allows you to save the articles to read them later.

In the Go-to-market slide, Buffer shows the integration with the main app, to access content, and this will reassure the investors that the execution is working and that the partners have accepted the integration. The slide shows a few clear data and a picture with an example of integration.

So in order to present a market entry strategy, it will be crucial to present a few key elements that would solve the main problems and overcome the challenge to adopt the product by the customers.

11.3 PERSUASION APPLIED TO GO-TO-MARKET

11.3.1 Credibility

You cannot learn Go-to-market from books or at university. This is the part when an entrepreneur will get his hands dirty and show what they can do. This is the part of doing business when the entrepreneur puts themselves to the test.

That is why the investors always appreciate people that already have experience in similar conditions. Who has already experienced failure or, possibly, the success of a Go-to-market strategy executed in accordance to all the rules.

If you already have had some experience, the way you speak changes, as well as the way you are perceived when presenting a new business. I recently saw this myself, supporting a very interesting start-up. The founder arrived, introduced himself and started explaining his project.

When he was talking, I realized that he was answering exactly all the questions coming to mind, and I felt like I was being lead through a clarifying route on all points.

When he presented the team slide, my attention was immediately drawn to the caption behind his picture. I was curious to know the founder's background. What I read was absolutely in line with my expectations: the founder was an entrepreneur with an exit behind.

When you have already experienced the mistakes of a Go-to-market and you have been able to overcome them, you already know the threats to pay attention to, and when you are presenting, this comes out naturally.

One more time, what is conferring credibility to the section is your team's expertise.

Moreover, the Go-to-market supports the credibility of other sections like the problem and solution, showing the existence of a need, and the customers will to pay in order to fulfill it.

11.3.2 Focus on the audience

Often, entrepreneurs take for granted that once the product is ready, the rest will follow. However, the execution is a crucial part of any entrepreneurial project, which will often lead to the failure of the whole start-up.

Investors already know that, and will always assess the entrepreneurs in great detail about their real potential to implement Go-to-market strategies, which are often too ambitious. If you had experience, you would become credible, and so the investor can believe you will be able to do it again, perceiving a lower risk and a higher return of their investment than that of a newcomer.

The fact that Buffer shows a slide where he says that 6 integrations had already been realized and that now two new ambitious partnerships are on the way, would allow investors to lower the perceived risk, just for the fact that they already had realized many partnerships.

Therefore, the Go-to-market is based upon perceived expertise and itself consists of a critical factor that will allow investors to lower the risk perceived by the investor towards your start-up.

11.3.3 Emotionality

Thinking of the Buffer case, previously shown, we could imagine the founder's story when proposing a pocket partnership.

Imagine the founder of Buffer recounting the day when he demonstrated the opportunity of partnership. He could tell how his presentation went, or even the reactions it caused.

Think of such a speech. *"We have presented the opportunity to integrate Buffer into the sharing panel of pocket contents. People were inattentive and were hardly following us, but then we launched a demo simulating the integration with Pocket. The audience jumped on their chairs, looking at our features integrated into their app. We didn't even have time to end our presentation before they wanted to know how to proceed with the integration".*

Coming back to us, you can easily realize the storytelling strength to support the Go-to-market. The stories, as we have seen in other sections, bring to life abstract concepts and when we are talking of people, the audience will naturally feel more involved.

11.4 Summarizing

A good Go-to-market strategy is at the basis of any start-up success. Having a good execution plan means having clear plan in our mind as to how to "make things happen".

However, the Go-to-market requires expertise. Seldom a market approach strategy comes from the improvisation and, as we saw, you cannot learn it from the books.

Any start-up requires an ad hoc strategy; there are no prepackaged models. The investors are aware of the importance of—and, at the same time—of the criticality of this section.

Be solid and convincing, experiment, apply tests and collect all the required metrics in order to identify the right route to bring your product/service to the target market.

CHAPTER 12

THE TEAM

> *"If you entrust a good idea to a mediocre team, it will ruin it. If you entrust a mediocre idea to a brilliant team, that team will improve the idea or will abandon it and will propose a better one"*
>
> **Ed Catmull,
> Founder of Pixar & Walt Disney Chairman**

> *"A start-up causes to the relationships among the founders what a dog causes to a sock: if he can destroy it, he will"*
>
> **Paul Grahm** [2]

I have always thought that people make the difference and in a start-up nowadays, this is even more true.

Paul Grahm counts among the most common 18 start-up causes of failure, the choice of having only one.[1]

P. Grahm argues that firstly, this choice could let outsiders believe that the founder hadn't been able to involve any of his friends, and, considering that his friends should be the people that should trust him, this is not a good sign with regards to the project.

Moreover, making a start-up is too hard for a single person. There always will be the need of some co-founders with whom to discuss the business trend, to brainstorming with and, possibly, just have a chat. Having co-founders on whom to focus allows the start-up to also have a support on which to count in difficult times.

When you are presenting your pitch, the investors won't only pay attention to the content, but to the way you are describing it. I am not only talking about public speaking, but of your impact, of your leadership, of your ability to be perceived as an expert entrepreneur.

A further important factor is represented by the relationships among the founders. P. Grahm argues that 20% of the start-ups that they financed lost at least one of their founders.

For this reason, one of the points of attention of any Combinator in the selection phase is the status of the relationships among the founders.

For the most, Paul states, *"The conflict could have been avoided if the things had been clear from the beginning"*.
Avoid involving your roommate in an entrepreneurial project just because it would seem bad for him to be excluded, and avoid involving someone with whom you disagree because you are afraid you won't find anyone with his skills anywhere else.

People are the founding element for the success of a company, therefore don't rush and dedicate to such topic the required time.

Upon the team slide, you will often play the whole presentation. A weakness in the product can always be improved; if the financial projections need to be corrected, the investor has the skill to help you; but if the team is inadequate for the difficult task to be fully realized, nobody could help you.

How to present the team. What are the crucial elements to surface for any member of your team? What way will the team lay out data connected to the rest of the pitch presentation in order to strengthen it?

---

[1] The 18 mistakes that kill startups, paulgraham.com

[2] What we look for in founders, paulgraham.com

12.1 SMALL AND WELL STOCKED

You may look at an early stage start-up, with a very small amount of cash and the need to realize, in a very short time, an MVP in order to survive. They are presented with teams of many members.

The problem does not arise in the number of people, per se, rather the superimpositions that happen among professional figures.

Often, in order to build up the first MVP and validate the basic hypothesis, a few well prepared figures are sufficient. Superimpositions generate wastage and wastage is not admitted in a start-up, especially if you are collecting funding from professional investors. Investors want to get the most return on investment possible; nobody will invest in order to finance a team consisting of friends that are part of the project just because they've known each other for a long time.

Avoiding wastage means to avoid superimpositions between skills and having only those professionals that are strictly required on the team. Remember that resources are costly, even in the initial stages. Hopefully the company's shares will increase in value.

Usually in a start-up, there should be two types of skills involved in the team: business skills and technical skills.

Imagine that you want to create a new social network and assemble a team consisting only of business profiles. Who will develop the product? In many cases, there is a tendency to think that a team of business profiles could easily engage some freelancers in order to develop the technical side.

Then, with the onset of the low-cost online freelancing marketplace, it's quite a common idea to hire freelancers in underdeveloped countries, paying them a low fare and letting them develop the solution.

Keep in mind that a product's technical development requires constant maintenance work. Moreover, especially in the initial stages, the start-up requires passion and devotion that would be impossible to locate in a freelancer.

In addition to that, working with external suppliers only motivated by cash flow will expose the project to very high risks. A start-up cash flow has usually very limited resources available and you won't be able to risk that. As soon as they have been exhausted, the technical team will abandon you.

The same thing is good for the businesses that take care of bringing the product to the market and acquiring new clients. These resources are crucial in planning, testing, and in the implementation of your business model.

A start-up consisting only of technicians could come up with a phenomenal product, but they could find themselves completely unable to bring it to the market.

You shall also consider that the investors are absolutely aware of the risk in investing into a start-up that does not have a complete team, and since the team is the founding base for a good solution and a good Go-to-market, not having a good team could result in a start-up with a cheap product or one that would totally be unable to approach the market.

People that do business and decide to professionally dedicate themselves to it have specific skills and must be extremely motivated.

This is one of the reasons why most investors are no longer interested in teams that are only working part-time on one idea.

Another critical aspect is the knowledge of the context in which you are operating. If you are developing a wallet for digital cryptocurrencies, it will be advisable to have at least one person with a good knowledge of financial and cryptocurrency topics in your team.

In the previous chapters, I have told you about my experience follow up on a start-up program that proposed a solution in the biomedical field. In most cases, the teams consisted of practitioners and biomedical engineers.

The knowledge of a sector represents a critical element for the team that decides to operate in it.

12.2 THE IDEAL TEAM SLIDE

The team is the foundation of any start-up, the main element of any entrepreneurial project's success and, as such, is crucial inside a pitch presentation.

The team must be presented carefully in a strategic way, and the contents of the slide, although obviously essential, must carefully support the other sections of the pitch.

In 2017, Siren Care won the TechCrunch Hardware Battlefield[3]. Siren Care develops wearable hardware devices that allow to monitor health parameters of the human body in real time. A product that can be taken as an example are the socks for diabetics that monitor the person's temperature in real time and are able to prevent problems by informing the patient when it is time to contact a doctor.

Figure 1 - Siren Care Socks

This is a hardware product that operates in the healthcare world. Therefore, it certainly requires you to have electronic skills, skills in the world of wearable devices, and it would help to have knowledge of the retail world, in order to distribute them on the market.

When the CEO, Ran, is introducing her team, she says, *"I have spent time as biomedical engineer and I took care of developing masks for facial reconstruction in the military field. Jie, our CTO, has got 10 years of experience as electronics engineer and has developed various hardware products. Henk Jan, our COO, has sold to the biggest groups in the world like Zara, H&M[…]".*

Listening to Ran, it seems that team was specially designed for their project. Everyone has a specific role with a solid background and specific skills. There are no overlaps in expertise amongst the members of the team. They all are essential.

Figure 2 - Siren Care team slide

Such a team can immediately make you think that there is everything you may need and that, even if the start-up may not have the traction yet, they will have a team with all the required expertise to understand the market, developing a quality product and selling it through major customers.

---

[3] Dillet R., And the winner of Hardware Battlefield 2017 is… Siren Care, techcrunch.com

Let's now get a look at the interesting Buffer example.

Figure 3 - Buffer's slide team pitch

This slide seems to be more complete than the previous one because, in this case, there also are advisors and investors. Starting from the top, the first two are members of the team and will clearly show the ability to realize an effective Go-to-market, and implement a successful business model.

In fact, Joel is the person that has lead the project from idea to revenue in just 7 weeks, while Leo has been able to increase the user base from 200 to 55,000 people.

To strengthen the team, there are two famous advisors and professional investors that already support the start-up.

Does it seem reliable? Do you believe that all this may have an impact on the investors' risk perception? I believe so.

Crew (formerly called ooomf) presents its team in a very effective and complete way.

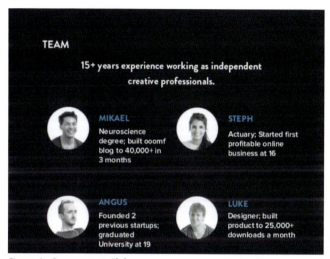

Figure 4 - Crew.co team Slide

First of all, as for the case of Siren Care, please note the presence of the pictures that create a positive and more personal effect compared to a slide that just has names. Some time ago, I attended a summit of digital marketing. They were introducing a company that was taking care of neuro marketing and digital communication sciences.

The speaker was presenting the case study of a website that had incredibly increased its conversion rate after having entered the pictures of their people on their landing page.

Do you remember in chapter 3, at paragraph 3.2.3, relating to the emotionality, I spoke about the persuasion strength that pictures of people may have on your pitch. I am quoting that part:

"It has been demonstrated that seeing pictures of people in which we identify ourselves generates serotonin. This mechanism is connected to the affiliation of a peer group that, since we lived as nomads crossing the Serengeti, is the basis of human survival.

This is the reason why pictures of people are used in order to reinforce the storytelling parts inside a presentation [...]".

Therefore, some advice would be to use pictures of the team members in order to make your presentation more convincing.

Later, as you can see in Siren Care's presentation, it is always better to identify the role of any member of the team. This will be useful in order to show that the team has all the necessary roles covered and that nobody overlaps with anyone else.

In addition to that, it is critical to show why, in function of the background and expertise, any member is absolutely fit to cover the position that has been assigned to him/her.

If I had to criticize Crew's slide, I would say that it is not clear who is the CEO and what role any team member fills.

Finally, as in the Buffer case, there could be some cases where the team consists of advisors, investors or other strategic members that are not part of the management team. In such cases, my advice is to show the people that add value to the team, but I invite you to always give them less prominence with regards to the management team, who should always stand out as the main resource.

12.3 PERSUASION APPLIED TO THE TEAM

12.3.1 Credibility

Competence is the basis of credibility, especially in the case of a team. If you develop a biomedical solution to make pharmaceutical companies' tests more efficient on some medications and you never worked in the biomedical world, nor do you know or are not involved with pharmaceutical companies, you will be seen as less than credible.

When you get the flu, would you rely on a doctor or an engineer? I know that this may sound banal if I am asking you such a direct question, but this is just what the investors are asking themselves when they invest in a team that has the know-how of the project's context.

Other elements that support your credibility are the team's motivation and commitment. How should you measure them? Through the initial investment. If one team has financed, even in a small part, the first stages of the project, this shows that people that work on the project believe in it so much that they are investing in it.

After all, why should an investor risk his financing if you're not willing to risk your own?

So, if this activity has been self-funded, don't hesitate to show it. It could only improve your credibility as a motivated entrepreneur.

12.3.2 Focus on the audience

In order to reduce the risk perceived by the investors, one of the most important things is to show a complete team. In general, it is alright to avail ourselves of external professionals in order to be helped in our job, but it won't be good to entrust the key parts of the project to external people that are more motivated by wage than by the entrepreneur's vision.

If you are developing software that would exploit the machine learning mechanisms to solve a problem in an innovative way and learn from the user's behavior, it will be critical to have an expert of machine learning as part of your team.

Developing an entrepreneurial project is extremely stressing, requires passion and determination, to work with no schedule for months or years on end, and often with no retribution. The entrepreneurs live in the hope and conviction that one day their start-up will be so good that they can have a comfortable future and, for this matter, are willing to sacrifice their present.

In this case, the dedication of the team to the project is critical to reduce the risk perceived by the investors. It must absolutely avoid presenting teams that manage their project as a secondary subject, to be managed on the side to their main job.

After all, a founder that is committing a good part of his time in his main job and is dedicating the remaining time to the start-up could deliver the impression that he himself does not believe it would be worth investing more time in the entrepreneurial project. If so, how could the investors be convinced to fund it?

The investors would think that you won't seriously bet on the project, and that if things are not going well, you could simply abandon ship. In addition to that, having noted the level of commitment that a start-up project requires, you won't be that credible, and this for sure would prevent you to collect funding.

12.3.3 Emotionality

I would like to tell you the story of a friend of mine, formerly a manager of an important giant of the web. This manager was an expert fan of recruiting. Every time he had to recruit a new resource, he used to study the selection interview in every detail.

However, there was one thing that had impressed me more than anything else: he used to say that asking generic questions on the applicant's profile would necessarily lead to receiving limited responses. The way to discover if an applicant really was fit to cover a certain role was to simulate the situation and immersing the applicant in the context, and then monitor their behavior.

The manager created plausible scenarios of critical situations to be managed, and asked the interviewed people to intervene.

This way, he was able to know, based on concrete behavior, who those people really were.

Imagine exploiting such technique in order to concrete the team's strength. When you present the team, you could tell a small anecdote where the team, solved a critical situation with collaboration, symbolic for the start-up success.

Try to use this technique in your start-up context, and think of how many critical situations your dream team overcame successfully. You have many stories to tell!

12.4 Summarizing

For many investors, the team is by far more important than the idea. During the pitch, the investors will often listen and evaluate the entrepreneur and his team.

A complete and experienced team represents the basis for the success of any entrepreneurial project. You will need motivation and commitment in order to cope with the rhythms and challenges imposed by doing business.

A valid team will allow things to happen, and concrete the business plan and entrepreneurial strategies.

Build the team slide, illustrating the roles and expertise of each team member in such a manner that they would complete each other, avoiding an experience overlaps. Always put a personal touch to the slide by adding nice pictures of every team member.

Remember: people make the difference.

CHAPTER 13

FINANCIAL PROJECTIONS

We are getting close to the end of your investor pitch, and the moment has come to talk about your business in such a way as to apply certain plans and strategies in a financial prediction that would allow the investors to understand the potential of their investment.

Planning of the financial resources is crucial for the sustainment of the business in the middle and long run.

> *"All the companies that fail have a common cause of failure: they have exhausted their financial resources"*
>
> **Don Valentine,
> Sequoia Capital**

An entrepreneur should have the ability to plan their business to manage it in a rational manner with a long period perspective, to not be influenced by everyday events, and to make the company look interesting to the investors' eyes.

Calculating the financial forecasts require time, and in order to maintain them, you will need it time again—especially when following the quick evolution dynamics of a start-up.

How do you make credible financial predictions? What elements make sense to present in an investor pitch? How far should you go with your ambitions?

13.1 REALIZE CONSISTENT PROJECTIONS

Financial projections reflect your strategies, your milestones, the functioning of your business model and the operation of the whole activity.

Firstly, you will need to be consistent. If you presented a certain Go-to-market strategy and a traction that would describe results and growth, the financial projections would certainly have to be in line with the other sections.
I realize that it could seem an unimportant recommendation, but I can assure you that when you start working on Excel to box in the financial projections figures, the risk of forgetting the connections with the rest of the presentation is very high.

This happens because, working among tables, you will focus a lot on the assumptions that would allow you to calculate, gradually, the following years. I have seen some start-up presenting financial models that were inconsistent with the traction metrics presented previously.

In short, it is alright to immerse your pitch in the detailed financial hypothesis, but always keep in mind everything that you have shown previously in order to remain consistent.

13.2 PREDICTING THE FUTURE IS NOT EASY

Realizing the famous financial projection table is a hell of a job for sure. It will require lots of work, great attention to detail and will especially require you to build figures on a thick base of assumptions that need to be defined.

How much your business will grow in the future? How would be the market demand be represented? Which demand percentage will I be able to fulfill? How would the market's demand evolve? Etc.

I could continue to ask countless questions to which nobody can give answers. This, however, cannot stop you because you have given estimates, and so you will just have to make some assumptions.

Usually assumptions are based on what that has happened in the past. In the luckiest of cases, the company has some metrics that would allow you to make assumptions; in other cases, that wouldn't be feasible. Right now, I am working on the financial projections of a start-up of mine that, by luck, has a couple of years of history, and so I have a base to start from.

For instance, if you know how the company has grown in recent years, you already know that there is a growth rate you will be able to achieve. Will it be sustainable then? It is up to your sensitivity and to your knowledge of your activity to establish the answer to that question.

Another difficult factor is that you will never know in detail how far you should go. If you estimate your employees, consider the wage increment for any type of contract year by year. They will affect the total cost structure.

Starting from the prerequisite that the metrics projected outside 18 months are, in practice, science fiction. If you have to explain the next 5 years, you should try to give a rough idea, without going into too much detail.

I have seen financial plans that were extremely detailed and complete, so rich in assumptions that the day of the pitch, at the first question from an investor, the entrepreneur couldn't remember the reasoning behind the assumptions that had brought him to certain results.

Considering that you and the investors are aware of the low truthfulness of revenue and cost projections by the fifth year, my advice is to work with simple figures and rough assumptions.

13.3 PROJECT YOUR AMBITION

With forecasts, you don't know what the investors are looking for; would it be better to have a very aggressive and ambitious plan, or to adopt a low key, reassuring and credible figures?

On one hand, we have the investors, who are clearly looking for realistic forecasts, in which the entrepreneur really believes. On another hand, we find investors that believe a start-up should not be that ambitious.

During one of the latest start-up competitions that I follow, I remember an investor in the jury who complained the start-up had been too ambitious in their projections, which without, they would not have been able to raise interest from the investors. because those financial models would hardly have allowed highly profitable investments.

After all, there are entrepreneurs that don't work in the context of mere profit, but just out of entrepreneurial passion. So there are some results that, even without aspiring to become the next Facebook, would deem them to be fulfilling anyway.

I remember an investor that funded a start-up in the eCommerce world. That start-up went very well, but, after some years, the growth grew steady and the entrepreneur was very happy to have stabilized at that level.

The investor was obviously not satisfied, because the greater the start-up was aspiring to grow, the greater his shares would add value. I remember the investor exclaiming, *"If all start-ups reasoned this way, investing in a start-up or in a mall in my district would yield exactly the same result"*. Who was wrong, the entrepreneur that had realized himself in his entrepreneurial vision, or the investor that was looking for more aggressive growth?

I firmly believe that entrepreneurship should be a passion, but I realize that, if a certain type of investor is involved, then they will have to assume the responsibilities of their own actions.

Having some investors on board necessarily implies that you will have to accommodate, at least in part, the requests. The investor is aiming for the exit, unless he is an angel that can become passionate about the idea, and decide to take part in it for other reasons.

Show ambition and do not hold back. This is one of the features your financial plan should meet. In fact, as I continue to say, we are all aware of the low probability of long-range forecasts, which allow you to plant your flag on a result you would like to achieve.

If you are presenting a start-up whose goal is to realize 80K€ at its fifth year, with 4 years of negative results before breaking even[1], it will probably not be an interesting start-up for an investor.

Research shows that the human brain reacts much better to the funding dimension than to the risk connected to it.[2] In short, large numbers, even with the potential and high risk, attract the investors' attention much easier than small numbers. Don't be scared to be ambitious. If you need an important funding boost, that would imply the intervention of an investment fund, you should present a suitable financial plan.

---

[1] Break even point of revenue and cost
[2] Peterson R.L., The Neuroscience of Investing: FMRI of the reward system, Stanford University

13.4 A MAP THAT CAN SHOW YOU THE WAY

Realizing financial projections is difficult and expensive, because it requires a lot of time from the entrepreneur and a constant application of effort.

Moreover, the start-up evolves at impressive speeds. Everything changes too quickly, and your five-year plan would remain reliable in the long term. Therefore, it is possible, that your projections would already be old only a month after being realized. You would therefore have to revise them upwards or downwards.

In short, these financial projections require time to be realized, and then time to be updated. This is because people will try to avoid making these calculations unless required by a contest or by a fundraising campaign.

In reality, having recently realized some of my own entrepreneurial activity, I noticed a great feeling of relief, some ambitious projections in front of me, and in which I believe.

Having an economic plan of the metrics, allowed me to understand if I was on the right track, and if I was going along it quite quickly. Since I was immersed in the business, and I am a human being, it was inevitable that my judgment would be misled at that moment, by the context, by emotions.

You may experiment with a strong increment of demands, and so you could accelerate the collection of resources, you could purchase computers and software licenses. In short, you could be investing in order to sustain your growth. In the short term, it could seem to be you doing this. You will seem to have gone too far, and you could ask yourself if it would really be the right moment.

However, if you have a long-term plan and you know that to realize such results, you should end the fiscal year with a certain organizational structure, then everything will look more rational and you can feel that everything would be under control.

Therefore, independent from a fundraising campaign, I strongly advise you to always have updated financial projections at hand. Did you end the first six months of the year in a good position? Good! Update the projections now that the first six months have been consolidated. This way, you will have a more reliable estimate for the first year. Use the financial projections like a GPS device, which can show you the way and the "minimum" speed limits to run over some roads.

13.5 PRESENT THE FINANCIAL PROJECTIONS

In the pitch, great evidence of slides related to the financial projections won't be presented. One example is LinkedIn's round B.

Figure 1 - LinkedIn financial projection

In this case, the table with all detailed revenues and costs up to the operating margin have been reported.

When you realize your calculations on the financial projections, you would present a table containing numbers, probably realized in Excel. This will be the most complete tool used to realize it. Despite the fact that a table is not the best manner to present all this data into a pitch presentation, it is the best for working out finances.

Investors are quite sensitive to these calculations and they want to analyse them in detail. If your pitch raises the interest you hope, there will be a diligence moment where you have all the time you need to explore the calculation with the investors.
During a pitch, my advice is to answer only the key questions an investor could ask, among which are:

1. What is your entrepreneurial ambition?
2. When will you achieve the break-even point?

Show a histogram that would project the margin's values and, in just one slide, you can answer both questions.

Moreover, during the pitch, you don't want interested investors stuck on the financial projection slide with detailed questions on the calculations. Your goal consists of finishing the presentation as fast as possible.

Avoid projecting all the details with your table, and it will also help you avoid uncomfortable questions.

My advice is to keep the slide with the table either hidden or held as backup. It could be useful if, having finished the presentation, more detailed questions are asked of you.

13.6 PERSUASION APPLIED TO FINANCIAL PROJECTIONS

13.6.1 Credibility

I invite you to be ambitious and I encourage you to present a quite aggressive financial plan because, in accordance to some research made in collaboration with Standford University. This will better attract the investors' attention.

Pay attention, however, I am not inviting you to present financial plans that have no connection with reality. The truthfulness of the projections decreases upon the increase of the provisional horizon; however, it will be critical that you really believe to be able to realize those metrics.

I realize that it would be impossible to ask you to swear on the truthfulness of the projections but, if you ask yourself, "Do I really believe in this financial plan, do I really believe that I could achieve those results?". The answer should be, "Absolutely, yes!", providing that the assumptions you define are met.

> *"Avoid creating financial projections to interest the investors. Instead, realize projections you really believe in"*
>
> **Marc Andreessen**

Be ambitious, but more than that, be honest with the investors. Integrity stands as the basis of credibility. If you have low integrity, you should be aware that, unless you are an excellent actor, the investor will work that out. They won't rise from their seats and shout "Dishonest,", but they will simply feel distrusting towards you that will create in them a negative perception of yourself.

According to Paul Grahm, the secret to really looking honest consists of being able to convince yourself of the truthfulness of what you are saying. If you propose an investment to strangers, the first thing that you should be convinced of is the investment truthfulness. If you are not, if you, in their place, would not invest, all this will be perceived and you will lose credibility.

Paul Grahm suggests, forgetting mind games and public speaking tricks, and focus on the calculations in order to demonstrate the truthfulness of the investment. If your calculations show that your investment is not valid, get back to work and forget fundraising for now.

More often, people collect in correspondence of fictitious deadlines, as for instance, the much-praised demo day. If you are not ready, wait, work on it and come back when you are seriously convinced of the truthfulness of your investment.

You will appear convincing and credible to your investors' eyes. How do you demonstrate the validity of your investment? According to Paul Grahm, the most important thing is that you be a real market expert.

If you aren't, the investors would need just few questions to discover that fact. Therefore, if you are not, start studying and thinking about honest and, therefore, credible calculations to present like real investment opportunities.[3]

---
[3] How to convince investors, paulgraham.com

13.6.2 Focus on the audience

Investors are looking for a high return with the minimum possible risk. A professional investor expects to realize at least ten times his investment when talking about a start-up.

This will give you the ability to understand if your predictions have been sufficiently ambitious in order to be able to stimulate an investor's interest.

Let's assume that a VC invested 1M€ for 10% of equity on your activity to year 1. After five years, your activity is billing 20M€ and one partner interested in the merge proposes to buy it for 100M€.

Assuming you sell, the VC would be entitled to 10% of 100M€, thus 10M€—ten times their investment of 1M€, five years previous.

This calculation is a very simple example on how to use the correct logics to understand how far you should go to realize the attractive revenue projection.

The perceived risk is instead connected to the costs structure. If the revenues projections are deemed acceptable, or are uncertain on the cost model, more precision will be required. You must be aware of the required costs of operating the business model.

Obviously, the costs will evolve as well, and it will be difficult to predict the figures. However, it will be important to show a costing model that highlights the cost of the growth, and what would be needed to keep your business together.

Finally, your ability to collect an interesting revenue projection and a complete cost structure will reassure the investor of the facts that you are a prepared entrepreneur with the ability to quantitatively plan your business.

13.6.3 Emotionality

Financial projections are an extremely logical passage. There are some authors that propose not using anecdotes, or to decorate the slides. However, in this case, I believe that this passage should remain on the logical side, and I would not recommend you any other type of distraction.

Therefore, remain rational and try to appear solid and credible in your presentation.

13.7 Summarizing

Realizing a good business plan that would lead to solid financial projections will allow you to demonstrate to the investor that you are able to plan your business, to track the course and to follow it.

Even well-structured financial projections, will be inaccurate. Nobody can predict the future!

Nevertheless, they are an essential tool to show the ambition of your start-up and show the investor a project that would aim to provide the desired outcome for investment.

Financial projections also play a key guiding role for your start-up management. Exploit them and keep them updated, for yourself and for your investors.

CHAPTER 14

CALL TO ACTION

A pitch presentation is built upon the concept of providing information to the prospective investors so that he they can decide whether to invest. In the various sections of a pitch, we try to answer any the possible doubts an investor may have of your investment. The point of view of famous investors has a significant impact on the structure of the pitch that we have laid down, and are worth following if you wish to succeed.

The investors' point of view allows you to identify the data they want to use to make their decision.

The Reciprocation Principle, by R. Cialdini, says that people feel more prone to give to those that have given them something.

Up to this moment, in your presentation, you portrayed the goal to get something back. Now is the right time to ask!

What should you ask for? How should you ask? How much should you ask for? How do you build an effective request?

14.1 ASK AND YOU WILL RECEIVE

In a start-up competition one year, where digital entrepreneurs alternated on stage, with 3 minutes available to propose their ideas.

That day, I was particularly curious to know the start-up they presented, because the context was a digital marketing conference, and I couldn't resist the idea of looking at the innovative solutions in a field I am very passionate about.

Unfortunately, no start-up impressed me much, and some were even out of context, in my opinion. However, at a certain moment, one presentation drew my attention.

The beginning was good, and the entrepreneur was not the first one to present, so he succeeded in winning a panel that was already tired. The entrepreneur followed quite a consistent structure, introducing the problem well, exploiting its momentum in order to introduce the solution. Later, he showed us some business metrics, something on the market and competition, and then ended it all.

Before he ended his presentation, I felt very curious to discover his requests and his motivation. I kept asking myself, *"How much would you need and for what purpose?"*. If he asked the right thing, in my opinion, he would have drawn the interest of the investors for a follow up.

Nonetheless, once he finished giving the presentation, the entrepreneur thanked everyone and left the stage before we could ask him any question. The staff called him back and asked him to go back on stage, in quite an embarrassing moment.

The first question from the audience was, *"So what are you looking for?"*. Here's how to destroy a wonderful pitch presentation!

Asking something is legitimate; there is nothing wrong with doing it. In fact, in a pitch presentation, it is critical. Nobody will do what you are expecting if you don't directly ask him to do it. The strength of the presentation, after all, lies in the fact that you stand in front of an audience, and at the end, be able to make your request, looking people in the eye.

So, even before preparing any presentation, an investor pitch or sales presentation, clearly describe what you want to get from the people you are talking to.

After all, a presentation with no request at the end is like an eCommerce page that does not have the Buy It Now button.

An Amazon page is the perfect balance between give and take with regards to the user.

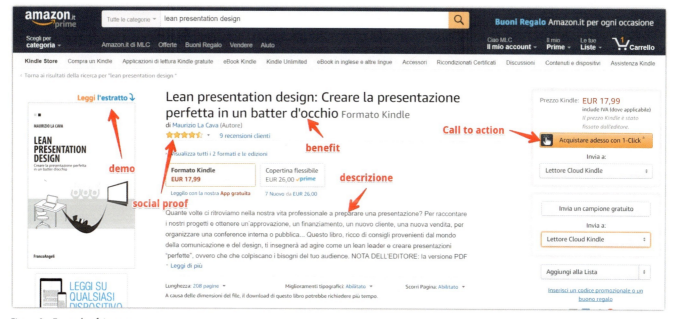

Figure 1 - Example of Amazon page

The call to action button stands out substantially with regards to the page, thanks to the fact that is filled with a particular color that contrasts against the background: the purchase button is orange.

The page has a title with a benefit that will motivate the user to buy; it allows you to read an excerpt of the text so that you can "taste" the quality of the content. It describes the product and then show you the reviews to prove the fact that others appreciate it. All these elements are needed by the user to clarify any doubt they may have, and help them understand if this is the product that they are looking for.

This concept is applied perfectly to the world of presentations. So, after you have given all the necessary data, now is the moment to ask for what you need.

14.2 WHAT TO ASK (REAL LIFE EXAMPLES)

Are you collecting funding, or are you looking for a strategic partner? Are you selling a product, or the company's brand during a new employer branding campaign, in order to get new applications?

Independent from the content of your request, this is the moment of the presentation where you put it forward in the most convincing manner.

In the case of an investor pitch, it is a funding application. It will therefore be plausible to expect a quantification of the call.

An explanation related to how the resources will be used is critical to reassure the investor hat you have the goal clear in your mind.

In the case of Airbnb, they are asking $500,000 in order to achieve 80,000 transactions, and so realize $2M in revenues. On the right side of the slide, they show how they will use their capital, and how they intend to invest the resources they collect.

The example of Fittr is better suited to explaining the allocations concept.

Figure 2 - Airbnb fund raising call

Figure 3 - Fittr shows how will the funding be allocated

Pay attention, though, because Aribnb is doing something more, not stopping at the application in absolute value. It also will explain the reasons.

Fittr's slide clearly shows the application, and then lists how the funding collected will be invested. My suggestion is to add another step and show the allocation percentages. This way, you will show the balance with which you will allocate the funding, giving a different importance to the various parts.

14.3 PERSUASION APPLIED TO CALL TO ACTION

14.3.1 Credibility

The whole presentation, if constructed well, has sided with you, trying to show you to be credible to the investors.

All the previous sections have the aim of showing off your skills and knowledge, and to convince the investors that you know what you're doing.

As you can see, this is the point of arrival at the end of a route you took many slides ago. The presentation is the route where you are accompanying, hand in hand, the investor towards the final call to action.

Along the route, you have let yourself know and to earn the trust of your audience. Now you have arrived at the end of the route, this is the moment of placing your request. Do you think you've done a good job, and that you are ready to ask?

If you don't, you should go back and reprocess your pitch until you absolutely feel at ease in advancing the funding application.

14.3.2 Focus on the audience

Knowing your own audience means also being able to properly interface. Entrepreneurs have the tendency to downplay themselves during fundraising, and to place themselves in a condition of inferiority, as if they were begging alms.

In reality, you, as entrepreneur, are offering an exceptional opportunity to your investors, the opportunity to jump on board your success train.

Don't be the first one not to believe in your entrepreneurial idea. If you don't, you won't be ready for fundraising. Go back to your calculations, build an investment that would really be interesting, convince yourself and then try to convince others.

If you are convinced of what you are doing, then this is the moment to stop thinking *"I'm asking for money"*, and begin to think *"I am offering a unique opportunity"*.

If you pay attention to Airbnb's slide, you will notice that, right after the application, there is the word "Opportunity". The message conveyed is therefore that it is an opportunity for the investors.

That slide has been constructed in a smart way, because it is showing how much investors can gain from the investment, and this will tease the investor, interested to maximize his profits.

The investment's allocations will instead reassure the investor that you carefully planned your funding needs by dimensioning a source of cost. In short, you should know what use you will make of what you are asking and that will prove that you will significantly reduce the perceived risk.

14.3.3 Emotionality

Binpress—marketplace to market open source solutions—is proposing itself with a slide for fundraising that is very interesting.

Figure 4 - Call to action binpress.com

The team could have placed "$200k" at the center of the slide and communicated, with no hesitation, their request. However, they are doing something different.

Instead of communicating the request in absolute terms, they presented it as the part of a funding route that is about to end.

Their message is not, "We need $200k", but, "There is still a small room for investing $200k to jump on board. But pay attention, there are many other people that are investing and that have already contributed for 80% of the required amount, you must act quickly if you want to be part of this investment opportunity".

This way of presenting is exploiting the effect of a combination of two phenomena: "Urgency" and "Scarcity".

Urgency is the feeling that something important is happening and, therefore, you should act quickly.[1]

It should clearly be something important for you. If you are booking a flight for the Canary Islands because you want to organize your holidays and, all of a sudden, realize that 15 people have booked today, 51 more people are buying in this moment, and the available places are ending (scarcity). You will realize that you must hurry up (urgency) to book if you don't want to risk to get the most convenient way to fly.

In the Expedia example below, you see that two popups appear in the low right corner, close to the call to action and pricing (visible position) that have the aim of making you rush.

---

[1] Patel N., How to use urgency and scarcity to improve conversions, crazyegg.com

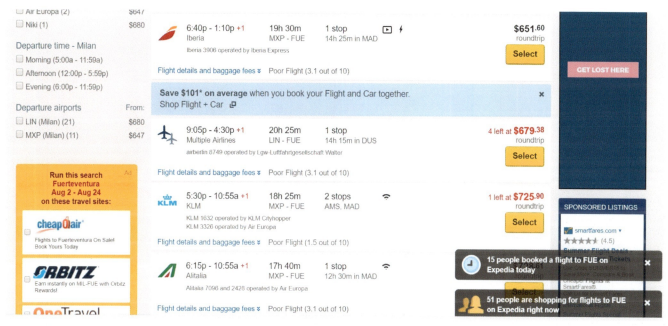

Figure 5 - Urgency effect on Expedia

Scarcity refers to any restriction on the availability of a product or service, with the aim of increasing the sales leveraging on the consumer. The fear of losing something causes people to act.[2]

What makes the scarcity concept interesting is that when something begins to terminate, people's desire to have that item begins growing.

The inverse relationship works like this:

• Maximum availability – nobody wants it
• Limited availability – everybody wants it

This technique is used a lot online to push consumers to purchase. An example, one that raises a state of anxiety in me is booking online. Every time I book a flight, it always seems to be the last one that has arrived and that, if I don't hurry up, I will lose the opportunity to be properly accommodated.

---

[2] Patel N., How to use urgency and scarcity to improve conversions, crazyegg.com

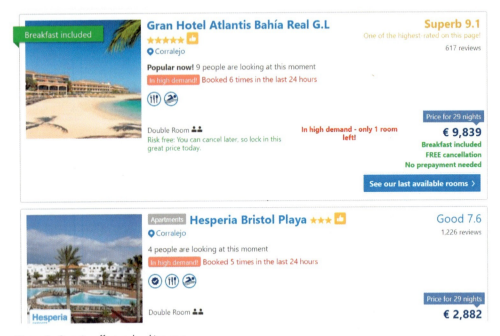

Figure 6 - Scarcity effect on booking.com

Every time I ask myself if the structure is really sold out or if the site booking is managing only a part of the existing rooms in the structure. That would mean that only a small part of the structure is being sold out. I often ask myself if it is true that they are being sold out, or if that is only a flag to create the scarcity effect.

You won't be able to know if that is true or not, so doubting and lose that opportunity, you will be profoundly affected by that feeling, that is pushing you to book before there will be nothing available.

Urgency and Scarcity are often used together. On one hand, you are told that people are booking, many people are booking right now. On the other hand, you are told that the places are running out. The obvious conclusion is that if you don't hurry up, you will risk finding no places available!

In the case of BinPress, their popups are different from Expedia's anonymous popups; they will give a name and a face to the investor.

As you can see, there are well-known brands and names. This is used to push you to think that if people that are so good and famous did invest, you are probably the one losing something. This is the classic mechanism of the reviews: if others are saying that the place is good, then it will be like that!
This is the mechanism of social proof, already defined in the third chapter.

This simple slide could seem completely harmless to anybody else, in reality, it has been designed in accordance to the best practices in order to persuade the investors to act and to act quickly!

14.4 Summarizing

The call to action is the final part of the presentation, the part where you, after having given so much, comes the moment to ask.

Specify what you are collecting, and show how you intend to utilize the raised funds.

Make your request in a clear and concise manner. Exploit the Urgency and Scarcity techniques in order to create an irresistible call to action that would prompt the investors to act quickly and to ask you for an analytical meeting.

CHAPTER 15

ROADMAP

Congratulations! You have almost completed your pitch. You have presented your great vision, with a bit of traction and an excellent business model.

In order to realize a great entrepreneurial design, you must begin somewhere. During the call to action, you submitted a funding application and shown how you intend to allocate, in percentage terms, the funds raised.

You explained "how much" and "how"; now you need "when"! What will you do first, and what later?

With which allocation will you start? That is, in what would you begin to invest the raised funds? Which goals would you set for the next few months, or years?

In short, in your opinion, how important is it to show your vision and to split in steps the route in order to be able to realize it?

15.1 ONE STEP AT A TIME

A start-up is an entrepreneurial experience animated by the farsighted vision of the entrepreneur. The vision is clear and well defined in the mind of the start-up creator, but, often and luckily, it is something quite futuristic.

In fact, as we saw, in order to realize a successful start-up, you should think of something that will be innovative in ten years' time, not today. Otherwise, over time dedicated to its execution, the idea will end up being outdated.

An entrepreneurial project is looking at the future, predicting the evolution of scenarios and trends, identifying a problem and a possible solution in a dynamic context that is quickly developing. It wouldn't be wise to develop an entrepreneurial idea you don't believe could work in the future.

To realize a long-range vision, keep the aim well fixed in your mind, to be able to draw a path to arrive there without losing yourself. In fact, the entrepreneurial path is full of dangers and unexpected things that can easily deviate you from the path you imagined.

Warning! I am not inviting you to be rigid; instead, be flexible and ready to readjust the trajectory of your path constantly in order to achieve your vision. However, have clear in your mind the goals to achieve, step by step, until the very last one, in order to be able to accept deviations that would, in any way, lead you to your destination.

The ability to plan a path full of goals, from the present to the future vision, requires a significant effort and great concreteness and to be able to succeed in this task you shall design a roadmap.

A traditional roadmap is a timeline that shows the required steps to achieve your vision, year after year. What characterizes it are the long periods of time that pass from one step and the other. Usually, the vision's roadmap is based upon yearly intervals at least, if not longer.

This is the typical roadmap used for CEOs' internal communications with the aim to show the path and the state of progress of the venture to the whole business team.

When I think of a vision roadmap, I'm thinking of a CEO that is presenting it on stage in front of a numerous audience of employees who need to know what the big boss has in his mind for the coming future.

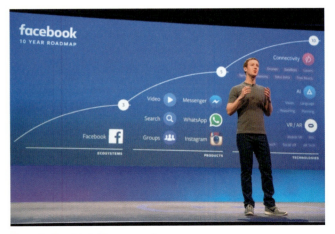

Figure 1 - Facebook 10 years roadmap

However, this type of roadmap is not that suitable to be used within your investor pitch. The investors know very well that most part of the estimates for the future have no worthiness and, most likely, they won't be met.

Think of what we said with regards to the financial projections for 3-5 years. It is well known that these are estimates with very low truthfulness. However, they are critical and the investor needs them in order to assess the chance to finance a start-up.

What would an investor be looking for inside a roadmap? One of the most important lessons that my professional experience has given me in the corporate world, and in particular my first marketing director, is what he used to call "managing expectations".

With these two words, he meant that I had been able to manage his expectations with regards to my work. A trivial example, if you cannot meet a deadline whatever the reason, the very first thing to do is be to inform and propose a B plan. You should act this way because in turn he will also be able to manage the expectations of his boss, and so on along the hierarchy.

At this point, the most effective strategy is the famous, "Under promise & Over deliver". That is, you should lower the expectations and surprise your interlocutor.

Imagine being a self-employed professional, the customer ask you to do A, B and C as soon as possible. You know that in order to realize all three of these, you will need 2 weeks. Then you negotiate with the customer a three-week delivery and then, once he accepted that, you start working.

The customer is waiting for a complete result at the third week, but you can deliver a complete work at the end of the second week. The customer will be surprised and happy. This trivial example explains in a very simple way the strategy mentioned above. Consider that to be just an example of the customer/supplier relationship, and never abuse this strategy.

Let's try to cover this relational dynamic in case of an interaction with the investor to whom you are asking to fund your start-up.

At the end of the pitch presentation, launch your call to action, with the aim to ask the investor for some resources, to allocate, as shown in the pitch, in order to make your start-up progress towards your vision.

The investor, by his side, could decide to fund your start-up but would like to know how will you manage the resources.

Same as the self-employed professional customer that is paying him to realize a project, the investor is funding you to let you develop your start-up.

The roadmap is the slide you show, in a temporal order; the goals (milestone) you intend to realize with the raised resources.

When you show a roadmap, you are committing to achieve some goals in a specific time frame. According to the above-mentioned strategy, the trick consists of remaining conservative and always taking more time with regards to what you really believe would be needed to achieve those goals.

The execution is one of the most ambitious parts of doing business. It will then be critical being able to introduce the progress and mark its times.

Engineers contend that in order to solve a complex problem, you will need to break it down into more simpler problems. This is exactly the rationale you should approach your entrepreneurial project's development project.

The roadmap is critical within a pitch in order to show how you intend to proceed, to convince the investor of your ability to manage a project and for yourself too.

The ability to plan in managing the entrepreneurial adventure is critical also and especially for yourself. The roadmap will act as a guide and will allow you to maintain your team in line with the future goals and on the deadlines to meet.

Marking times is critical in order to manage the efforts. Knowing that there are deadlines that shall be met, your team will work according to the timelines, or they will work hard at the very end, but in all cases, they will be aware of when to push hard to achieve the goal in time.

15.2 PRESENTING THE ROADMAP

Of all the pitches examined, the first one below is showing some interesting elements to capture in a roadmap slide is for sure the Buffer case.

![Buffer milestones slide showing: Launched web app January 2011; 55,000 users ($150K revenue) October 2011; Launch the API October 2011; Integrated in 50 apps December 2011; 100,000 users ($288K revenue) January 2012; 1 million users ($3.6M revenue) January 2013]

Figure 2 - Buffer's roadmap slide

Buffer, in a very simple way, has combined products development elements (Launch of the web app, launch of the API) with the users growth and the impact on revenue. This slide gives an insight that by launching the API, it will be possible to integrate the product with external applications and therefore we will set our goal in realizing 50 applications by December 2011.

Thanks to this strategy, 100k users and $288k in revenue is expected by 2012. The growth will then go on in an aggressive way with farsighted out come from January 2013 of the following years.

Pay attention also that some of the dates are marked in gray and others in green. This difference leads one to think that some represent milestones already achieved, others have yet to be achieved.

I believe it to be quite effective to show the outcome achieved and how they are functional to the achievement of the following ones. By showing the outcome already achieved, it will look more credible for the start-up to achieve all the following steps.

The Intercom case allows me to show you an example of how I would like you not to create a roadmap.

what we're looking for

* $600k convertible note
* 18 months of runway to work on:
   - product-market fit
   - customer dev
   - early marketing efforts
   - profitability
* Plan to raise further round in 12-18 months to turn up heat on marketing

Figure 3 - Intercom roadmap & fundraising slide

In fact, as you can see, in this pitch the data relating to the amount of funds required are mixed with the allocations and then there is a small remark on the next fundraising campaign.

Nothing on what will happen meanwhile is shown. Naturally, some questions will arise, as well as doubts concerning the way the company will try to reach the following fundraising round.

Unfortunately, it often happens in some pitches that a great confusion between the request for necessary resources and their allocation with data related to the roadmap is visible in their pitches.

The call to action is exclusively intended for the request and to show the allocations, while the roadmap presents the goals we would like to achieve over time. My advice is to never mix these two slides because, although supplemental, they perform quite different functions.

The last example I would like to show you is Mapme's case.

From this slide, we can certainly learn something, visually-speaking; however, I think it is too concise on the goals described.

In fact, the idea of a roadmap perceived as a timeline that starts from the left side to the right is quite conventional and, in presentations, conventional things help people to immediately perceive meaning and contents.

However, compared to Buffer's slide, this seems to be more abstract and less interesting. Looking at the slide, would you believe that Mapme's team could really achieve those goals? I think it would be difficult to give an answer, since the goals are very generic, it does not show the outcome already achieved, and no figures of any kind are shown.

Figure 4 - Mapme roadmap slide

15.3 PERSUASION APPLIED TO THE ROADMAP

15.3.1 Credibility

A 10 year roadmap result will be hardly credible, and will lead you to think that you had no experience in the execution. Remember that the roadmap is not a slide like all others, because different from the rest of the pitch, this is a slide that is representing your commitment.

So you should responsibly commit yourself on something you know are able to realize. As such, my advice is to reduce the time horizon as far as possible, and to show a roadmap that will present the progress in the next 12 - 18 months maximum.

I have recently supported a group of start-ups competing for a seed fund with 3 acceleration months. Some start-ups showed up with the traditional 5-, or in some cases, 10-year roadmap.

My advice has been to show which goals the entrepreneurs would like to achieve in the three acceleration months had they won.

The panel should have invested in the team that, more reasonably, would have shown interesting potentials at the end of the acceleration program and that, as a consequence, could have exploited, at best, the three months of support. As a consequence of this zoom on the three months, I suggest showing what would have happened if, at the end of the first 6-12 months and so on up to the end of the first 18 months.

In order to be credible, I believe it critical to work on the time horizon by decreasing it or expanding it in a reasonable manner, according to the goals you aim to achieve with the resources you collect.

Finally, making reference to the examples shown in the previous chapter, you should have perceived the string difference existing between Buffer and Mapme. So, Buffer was quantifying, with users and revenues, the progress achieved and the one expected, providing more credibility to its milestones.

Mapme instead was proposing generic, high level goals without going into too much detail, and this made it look less credible.

Never overlook the importance of data to be credible and, more than anything, focus on the strength of your traction and, consequently, of the outcome already achieved as a proof of the fact that you may achieve future goals.

15.3.2 Focus on the audience

The roadmap itself is a section of the pitch used to direct the presentation towards the audience's needs. In fact, through a roadmap, you will show the outcome an investor could expect, the dates and resources, within a certain time limit.

From the point of view of those that are making the start-up, all investors seem to be strange entities that do not comprehend our genius. From the investors' point of view instead, people that create start-ups seem not to comprehend the importance of listening to those that have more experience and know how to properly fund them.

During one of my presentations to an investment fund, I remember that one of the main problems I identified with the start-up was connected to the post financing communication.

We were using a cloud tool that was collecting all our investments, and thus the funded start-up, and for any start-up, it was possible to see their detailed metrics.

It was critical for us to show the progress of our portfolio to the funds' customer/investors. We generated newsletters showing how the eCommerce investments, for instance, had been performing compared to those in social networks.

The problem consisted of the fact that the tool we were using was an excellent instrument for viewing and aggregating existing contents.

We had to ask the start-up to enter the data periodically inside the tool. But the start-ups have already lots of things to do while trying to survive, you can imagine how much time they have to fill up long metrics forms for their investor.

It is not my intention to take sides at all, because I understand the needs of both parts, but I would like to highlight the criticality of the communications between investors and funded start-ups.

In fact, one of the activities that, as investors, was using much of our time was to chase the start-up and trying to understand their progress status in order to have a portfolio as complete as possible. In some extreme cases, some start-ups would disappear for months on end and will come back the day they had finished their cash.

You will certainly understand that using a roadmap during a pitch is like showing commitment towards achieving common goals. It would be just like saying that you commit yourself to use the collected resources to achieve some goals in a specific time frame.

This way, the investor knows what to expect from you and from the progress of your project. He could get in touch with you and realize if you are in line with the plan or if there has been something unexpected, in practice in any moment of the activity.

This will allow to reassure the investor, making him perceive a decisively lower risk. However, as we have seen, the investor would like to perceive a high performance, and thus it is imperative that you create an ambitious roadmap.

Therefore, you should try to balance a credible roadmap, on which you feel you could commit yourself with an ambitious plan that would showcase your execution speed. Always try to operate within the limits of credibility.

15.3.3 Emotionality

In order to add colour to a roadmap and involve the audience, in my opinion, the most effective way is to bring to life a specific future step.

If, for instance, you have recounted the story of the interaction of one consumer with your solution while attempting to solve his problem, in the initial stage, it could make sense to connect to the solution proposed today and show how it could change in the future when it is fully consolidated.

Imagine telling the evolution of the story presented at the beginning of the pitch, but projected in the future, after having achieved specific milestones of your roadmap.

Bringing to life the future of your company in the ending stage of the pitch could generate the effect of a grand finale during a presentation.

You could also think of bringing to life a vision that is even very far in time. However, my advice is to remain credible and focused on an audience that aims to perceive a low risk.

You should exploit the power of the stories in order to make your audience live an experience connected to a goal that their resources could truly allow you to achieve.

15.4 Summarizing

The roadmap is the pitch section where you are showing your commitment in a short- and long-term for using the resources you are collecting. This way, you are reassuring the investor and also providing them a parameter that would let him monitor the project's state of progress.

Thanks to a good roadmap, the investor will know what to expect from you in the next few months. You should thus focus on the contained forecasting horizons and show the goals, even in quantitative terms, in order to increase the credibility and impact of the message.

A good roadmap will allow you to lead your project, keep your team in line, and reassure the investor.

CHAPTER 16

END WITH A "CONTACTS" SLIDE

In the benchmark structure, if you are paying attention, you will see that the last recommended section is the part related to contacts.

I did not think to dedicate a whole chapter to this section, but I believe that it would be critical to mention it at least in this final recommendation compendium.

During pitch competitions, I often see the investors in the audience would photograph the last slide, in order to be able to use the information in order to make a follow-up and get in touch with the start-up later on.

I happened to receive some pitches that had no contacts listed, and I couldn't possibly know how to asking for an elaboration on their pitch once they left the stage.

In general, my advice is to always have a last cover, with your logo, your branding and contacts to close your presentation.

16.1 INVESTOR PITCH CANVAS

Working to realize your pitch can require a lot of time and, as you know well, entrepreneurs don't have time to waste.

There are even extreme cases of entrepreneurs that state they not to have time to waste on fundraising. However, taking time to collect the resources for your own entrepreneurial activity is one of the main tasks of an entrepreneur, so you should accept it and start working on it.

This does not necessarily mean that you should waste lots of time creating your investor pitch.

In this book, after providing an effective structure, I am also providing a further instrument that will allow you to save time and to enter all the necessary data to show investors.

Let me introduce you to the model called "The Investor Pitch Canvas".

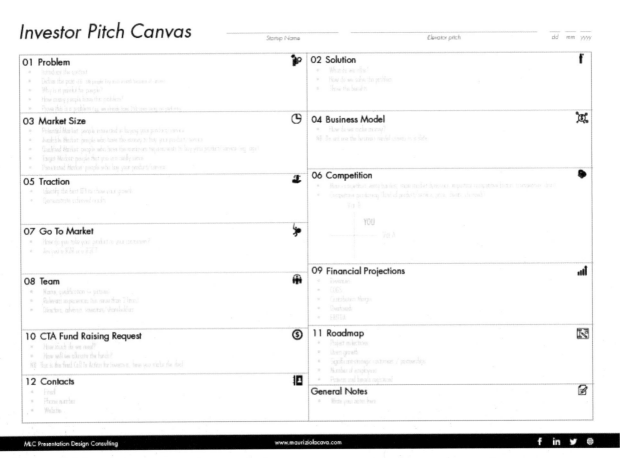

Figure 1 - Investor Pitch Canvas

This chart allows you to face the construction of a pitch in a structured way. In fact, the first thing to notice is the order in which all the sections are scattered. This is the order of the sections of the pitches. Thanks to the prioritization of the sections you shall no longer raise the problem of the information flow.

Moreover, as you can see, this model includes all the sections that should be contained in a pitch. It will be sufficient to follow the chart in order to prevent forgetting anything.

This model, moreover, is an excellent tool for brainstorming and constructing a pitch. In fact, the good presentation of a pitch includes a complete overview of the business activity, as it will necessarily affect the jurisdiction of various people of the team.

For this reason, the definition of the pitch contents represents the joint effort of more team members. The canvas will allow to work with several authors in order to collect everybody's contributions and allow them to receive credit for their parts.

For teamwork, my advice is to print it in large format, hang it on a wall and use the post-its.

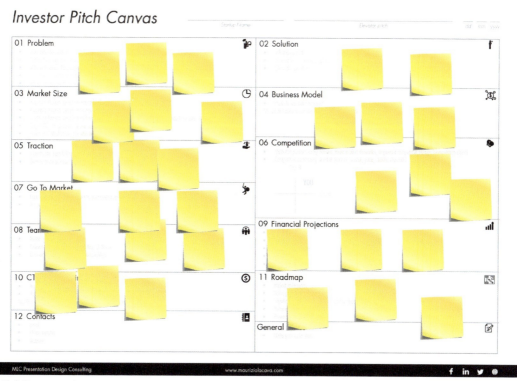

Figure 2 - Investor Pitch Canvas used to cooperate

This way every member of the team could add his contribution and the total amount of contributions will be already organized in a communication flow defined by the canvas.

So, once you have all the contents ready and already laid down in orderly manner, you will just need to make a work of synthesis for every section in order to decide what data the slide should contain.

16.2 THE ROLE OF GRAPHICS IN A PRESENTATION TO THE INVESTORS

Some start-ups assure me that they won't waste their time creating a pitch, because they will download a ready-made online form and enter the contents into it.

To create a good pitch, like for any presentation, first of all, you should build solid foundations. Create an effective communication structure.

This is the reason why I have provided an effective structure, obtained from the examination of hundreds of real-life cases and sector influencers.

Now you just have to cover the proposed structure suitable for the specific case with the contents of your project. So far, I haven't spoken about graphics, but structure and contents. In short, you should start focusing on what to say and not say, including all essential information for the investors.

Concerning the view of contents, you have two alternatives: you can let a professional do them, or you can do them yourself.

In the event of a professional, pay attention to the traditional approach used in the graphics and applied to the slides. In fact, any graphic designer that creates a layout of the slides as he would create a layout for a magazine using templates and InDesign, will not help you much.

What you need is a graphic designer that will reflect on the contents and combine the design with the message in order to create some layouts that will communicate the meaning of your contents.

If you decide to do it yourself instead, my advice is to keep your slides as simple as possible. Don't write too much, and focus more on speaking.

I will give you only one rule to comply with: "The speaker must always say more things than the slide, never the opposite".

If the speaker is providing more information in his speech than that on the slide, the audience's attention will be directed to him. If the slide is providing more information than to the speaker, the audience will lose sight of his speech and will try to read the information contained in the slide instead.

The reason most people fill slides with content is that we feel compelled not to say a lot verbally, and so have the tendency to include all the information we don't have time to tell into the slides. This is one of the most common mistakes that presenters make!

So, if you decide to make the slides by yourself, my only advice is to use extremely light slides and to focus on being complete in your speech.

GET YOUR FREE

HOW TO GET YOUR BONUSES

go to amazon

write a review

send the screenshot
info@maurizioIacava.com

BONUSES

1  THE ORIGINAL INVESTOR PICH CANVAS IN PDF AS EXPLAINED IN THE BOOK

2  POWERPOINT TEMPLATE OF EKOODO TO START WITH A WELL DESIGNED AND EASY TO USE POWERPOINT TEMPLATE FOR YOUR PITCH

3  A SET OF 8 INTERVIEWS OF PROFESSIONAL INVESTORS, VC, BUSINESS ANGELS AND PUBLIC SPEAKING COACHES TO BE EVEN MORE EFFECTIVE WHEN THEY DELIVER THE PITCH

Bibliography

- Berscheid, E., & Reis, H. T., Interpersonal attraction and close relationships, 1998
- Blank S., The Four Steps to the Epiphany, K&S Ranch, 2013
- Cialdini R., The Psychology of Persuasion, 2003
- Coughter P., The art of the pitch, Palgrave Macmillan, 2012
- Cremades, A., The art of startup fundraising, 2016
- Damasio A., Descartes' Error: Emotion, Reason, and the Human Brain, Penguin Books, 2005
- Dr. Abela A., The Presentation, CreateSpace Independent Publishing, 2010
- Duarte N. Reasonate - Present visual storied that transform the audiences, Wiley, 2010
- Fitzpatrick R., The mom test, CreateSpace Independent Publishing, 2013
- Kawasaki G., The art of start, Penguin Group USA Inc., 2004
- Kawasaki G., Reality check, Penguin Group USA Inc., 2011
- La Cava M., Lean Presentation Design, Franco Angeli, 2017
- Lipp C., The startup pitch, 2014
- O'Leary C., Elevator Pitch Essentials: How to Get Your Point Across in Two Minutes or Less, The Limb Press
- Patel N., Puri R., The Complete guide to understanding consumer psychology
- Ries E., The lean startup, Crown Publishing Group, 2011
- Rosenzweig P., The Halo Effect, 2014
- Saletti A., Neuromarketing e scienze cognitive per vendere di più sul web, Flaccovio Editore, 2016
- Sinek S., How great leaders inspire everyone to take action, Green Penguin, 2009
- Souza Homen De Mello F., Hacking the starutp pitch, CreateSpace Independent Publishing, 2014
- Justin Mares Gabriel Weinberg, Traction: A Startup Guide to Getting Customers, S-curves Publishing, 2014

Sitography

- http://mag.ispo.com/2015/01/90-percent-of-all-purchasing-decisions-are-made-subconsciously/?lang=en
- http://paulgraham.com/convince.html
- http://paulgraham.com/startupmistakes.html
- http://startupfundraising.com/38-startup-pitch-decks-from-companies-that-changed-the-world/
- http://www.astronautforhire.com/2013/04/insider-tips-on-nasas-astronaut.html
- http://www.investopedia.com/articles/personal-finance/102015/series-b-c-funding-what-it-all-means-and-how-it-works.asp
- http://www.investopedia.com/exam-guide/cfa-level-1/alternative-investments/venture-capital-investing-stages.asp
- http://www.isc.hbs.edu/
- http://www.paulgraham.com/fundraising.html
- http://www.startup-marketing.com/the-startup-pyramid/
- http://www.visualcapitalist.com/chart-5-tech-giants-make-billions/
- http://www.wheelofpersuasion.com/about/about-bart-schutz/
- http://www.ycombinator.com/
- https://blog.producthunt.com/
- https://conversionxl.com/emotional-persuasion-guide/
- https://growthhackers.com/growth-studies/airbnb
- https://guykawasaki.com/the-only-10-slides-you-need-in-your-pitch/
- https://medium.com/startup-grind/all-the-public-startup-pitch-decks-in-one-place-7d3ddff33bdc
- https://medium.com/startups-and-investment/the-importance-of-the-founding-team-82fdf7121a27
- https://techcrunch.com/2014/07/28/the-most-important-factor-of-startup-success/
- https://www.alexanderjarvis.com/2015/05/19/pitch-deck-collection-from-vc-funded-startups/
- https://www.crazyegg.com/blog/urgency-scarcity/
- https://www.entrepreneur.com/article/197560
- https://www.entrepreneur.com/article/229995
- https://www.entrepreneur.com/article/270515
- https://www.entrepreneur.com/article/270853
- https://www.forbes.com/sites/adigaskell/2015/11/04/why-the-wider-team-are-crucial-to-start-up-success/#d5a8cb36e4fe
- https://www.forbes.com/sites/andrewweinreich/2016/07/20/how-to-create-a-defensible-market-size-for-your-startup/#13b409be4cb1

- https://www.forbes.com/sites/martinzwilling/2012/05/20/startups-are-all-about-the-execution-so-tell-me-how/#366107f65fa7
- https://www.inc.com/geoffrey-james/how-to-give-a-flawless-elevator-pitch.html
- https://www.inc.com/mark-suster/the-importance-of-teams-and-why-the-best-leaders-cultivate-them.html
- https://www.psychologytoday.com/blog/inside-the-consumer-mind/201302/how-emotions-influence-what-we-buy
- https://www.quicksprout.com/2017/02/08/without-emotional-advertising-your-landing-page-wont-work-heres-how-to-get-it-right/
- https://www.slideshare.net/UTR/how-to-pitch-a-vc-dave-mcclure
- https://www.ted.com/talks/david_s_rose_on_pitching_to_vcs
- Nancy Duarte: The secret structure of great talks
- Simon Sinek: How great leaders inspire action

University papers and articles

- Bechara A., Damasio H., Damasio A., Emotion, decision making and the orbitofrontal cortex, Department of Neurology, Division of behavioral Neurology and Cognitive Neuroscience, University of Iowa College of Medicine, Iowa City, USA, 2000
- Conger J. A., The Necessary Art of Persuasion, Harvard Business Review, 1998
- Garner R., What's in a Name? Persuasion Perhaps, Sam Houston State University, Journal of Consumer Psychology, 2005
- Garner Randy, Name similarity and persuasion, Sam Houston State University
- Elsbach K, How to pitch a brilliant idea, University of California, Davis, 2003
- Hellman T., Financial projections for startups, University of Oxford, 2014
- Jason A. Colquitt, Brent A. Scott, and Jeffery A. LePine, Trust, Trustworthiness, and Trust propensity: A Meta-Analytic Test of Their Unique Relationships With Risk Taking and Job Performance, University of Florida, 2006
- Natasha D. Tidwell, Paul W. Eastwick, Eli J. Finkel, Perceived, not actual, similarity predicts initial attraction in a live romantic context: Evidence from the speed-dating paradigm, Texas A&M University and Northwestern University, 2012
- Peterson R., The neuroscience of investing: fMRI of the reward system, Brain Research Bulletin, 2005

Printed in Poland
by Amazon Fulfillment
Poland Sp. z o.o., Wrocław